Pick Up
Your Couch
and Walk!

Pick Up Your Couch and Walk!

How to Take Back Control of Your Life

PETER M. KALELLIS

CROSSROAD · NEW YORK

1994

The Crossroad Publishing Company
370 Lexington Avenue, New York, NY 10017

Printed in the United States of America

Library of Congress Cataloging-in-Publication Data

Kalellis, Peter M.
  Pick up your couch and walk! : how to take back control of your
life /Peter M. Kalellis
    p. cm.
  Includes bibliographical references.
  ISBN 0-8245-1378-9 (pbk.)
  1. Self-help techniques. 2. Self-reliance. 3. Health.
  I. Title
BF632.K35 1994
158'.1—dc20   93-21288
                                                         CIP

In loving memory of my beloved friend
Zeus
whose extraordinary presence provided
companionship, delight, excitement, and laughter.
Above all, he provided unsolicited
affection, enjoyment, and warmth
for fifteen solid years

To all my teachers,
from the first grade
to the last year of graduate work,
and to my supervisors
who patiently taught me
the craft of psychotherapy

and

To my patient clients,
students, and supervisees
who throughout the years
accepted my presence in their lives

My deepest gratitude
to my friends and colleagues,
Thomas A. Adams, Kyriaki A. Fitzgerald,
Christine Prevost, and Margery Hueston,
who painstakingly read, edited, and offered suggestions
for the completion of my original manuscript

Contents

Introduction

What can a book offer? Self-help books, like boosters, temporarily lift a person's psyche, providing comfort and options during the reading time. In a crisis, any knowledge or memorization of data or directives or rational injunctions can be of little help. They can hardly reduce the pain. But what really makes the difference is when we delve into our own soul and discover a way to self-autonomy and mature strength.

This is not a how-to-do-it book. The reader does not have to create an imaginary soul, a psyche. The psyche is already there. It has kept you alive thus far. But if it is currently tormenting you, you need to know what mysterious factors alienate you or seem to block your peace. If you feel trapped in the struggle for prestige, recognition, and appearances, you are probably a victim of wishful thinking. Concepts of what *should* be or what *ought* to be or how society, government, and the world should be — all these are mind mechanisms that lead into fantasy.

During the last forty years, psychotherapy, a tedious and expensive road to self-recovery, has branched out and blossomed in our society, promising solutions to life-long problems. Unquestionably, many have benefited by therapy of one sort or another. "Different strokes for different folks" is an adage that works for all.

A couple of years ago, *Newsweek*, in a cover story on support groups, noted that some fifteen million Americans attend some kind of self-help or support group, many of them based on the Twelve Steps of Alcoholics Anonymous.

Many people who join Twelve Step programs never question their sponsors. They memorize worthwhile axioms and the Big Book, not necessarily understanding their deeper meaning. At

times, sponsors or therapists are rigid, authoritarian, controlling, and shaming, but most attendees are hesitant to express
their feelings because they don't dare to challenge the authority
figure who supposedly knows the answers and has everyone's
best interests at heart.

The biggest single obstacle that keeps us within a neurotic
belief system is a written or unwritten rule that forbids us to
think for ourselves, to doubt, or to question beliefs and practices
that are contrary to human values.

As the end of the second millennium approaches, I have noticed in my practice an increase in the number of clients; the
prediction that by the year 2000 eight out of ten people in the
United States will have been exposed to some type of psychotherapeutic experience is not unrealistic. Psychotherapy, once
reserved for special cases and now in vogue for everyone, looks
more and more like the thing to do.

Some of the basic problems that propel people to psychotherapy are:

- anxiety

- boredom

- conflict

- depression

- disappointment and dissatisfaction with life

- emptiness

- fear

- guilt

- hunger for spirituality

We could add a symptom for every letter of the alphabet and
still leave out a few more symptoms. But there is one concept
that most psychotherapists believe to be true: that under each
symptom lies the deepest need of all, a cry for love.

Every year therapists encounter clients, young men and
women, married and single, who have had all sorts of ther-
apies — Freudian, Adlerian, Horneyan, Sullivanian, Rogerian,
Eriksonian, or an eclectic approach — to solve their particular

problem, but they remain dissatisfied with the results. There must be something missing in the treatment.

A world in which people cannot help themselves and improve their condition is unthinkable. To whom shall persons turn if they cannot trust themselves? Are they doomed to face life waiting for some outside salvation that may never come? Are most of us doomed to futility because not enough professionals are around to rescue us from our own wrong choices? Is there some way that we can use our own existing means to help ourselves?

If God's creation is so perfect and continues its life cycle with such accuracy and wisdom, did God also provide a factor within each human being that promises salvation? How we answer this question is our personal choice.

"Get deeper into yourself and learn from yourself what you must do," claims an ancient adage. Jesus of Nazareth was of the same opinion when he said, "The Kingdom of Heaven is within."

Teachers of all times seem to agree that persons cannot turn to someone else to save themselves, for the answers lie within their own reach and in their own inner endowments. I am not ignoring or opposing the mentor, the teacher, the therapist, the spiritual guide who facilitates recovery — all are members of the healing professions. But in essence, each of us has been given the medicine with which we can cure ourselves. It would be an unjust world indeed if this were not the situation.

The pool of Bethesda, which lay by the Sheep Gate in Jerusalem, was surrounded by a multitude of invalids — blind, lame, paralyzed — who awaited the moving of the water, for at certain seasons an angel came down and troubled it. The first person to step into the pool after the disturbance was healed of his or her disease. Among the crowd was a man who had been ill for thirty-eight years. Jesus approached him and asked, "Do you want to be healed?" There are few among us who would reply "No" to such a question. However, it should be pointed out that the one in pain needs to be willing to cooperate with the process of healing. The paralytic, suffering from the frustration of his situation, replied, "Sir, I have no man to help me."

"Get up. Pick up your bed and walk," Jesus said, empowering the patient to do so.

The above episode demonstrates the existence of the power

and will in each of us that, if we choose, will enable us to exercise our initiative and shoulder responsibility. The miracle inspired the title of this book, *Pick Up Your Couch and Walk!*

God, nature, built into each of us self-healing powers, at both the physical and psychological levels. Health is the natural state of being, and it restores itself when *we refrain from habits that interfere with it.*

In the physical world, technology takes over immediately to provide us with miraculous results. But when we hurt emotionally and we are psychologically disturbed, very little can be done. Authorities may make options available, but they seldom relieve our daily pain. We lose confidence in professionals when our emotional problem does not subside. When things get too hot to handle, we run in many directions, we escape into fantasies; some of these methods of coping can be self-destructive.

If life seems like driving in the face of oncoming traffic, we have to steer easily without panic; otherwise we risk damage. We need to develop *full trust in our own inherent capacities* and not flee in consternation from the scene.

We all have an intuitive feeling that we have a central core that is not ill and cannot be touched by the evils that haunt it. We are all aware that besides our physical self, with all its capabilities, there is a spiritual reality that keeps us alive and mobile. Let's call it *soul, psyche.* The question is: *Can this part of our humanity grow to maturity equally as well as the physical self develops?* Here lies the dilemma. Many of us nurture our bodies and maintain physical fitness; we take vitamins; we exercise. But how many of us try to nurture our soul? Do we know how? What prevents us from developing our own psyche, this inherent gift from birth? Where are we to look for the answer? To external sources? Or can we gradually find it within ourselves?

The task may be to learn to watch that spark of light that lies in your psyche rather than viewing the radiance of authorities or sages.

Chapter 1

The Self Rediscovered

In a world of conformity, where society expects us
to fit the mold if we are to be accepted, a human
being suffers immensely to establish a self that is
genuine and authentic.

—*Willard Beecher*

Sam Keen and Anne Valley-Fox, in their book *Your Mythic Journey,* point out that each person consists of at least three selves: the public self, the private self, and the unknown self.

The *public self* performs for an audience, real or fancied. It is the creation of the eyes that watch it. We learn to put on masks and costumes and play the roles society expects of us. Most of us avoid admitting that we conform to societal expectations, but we live in a world of reality and we need social approval to some degree.

The *private self* is a complex world of secrets in all sizes and shapes: fear, despair, disappointment, guilt, impotence, poor self-image, thoughts and actions that we are ashamed of. Also, for personal reasons, we hide ambitions, plans for the future, dreams, and fantasies. At times we allow friends, lovers, or family members to cross the boundary of our privacy. There is, however, an inner sanctum, the private self that no one enters.

The *unknown self* is the part of us that we discover daily as we experience the world we live in. It consists of experiences, feelings, fantasies, and possibilities that we repress rather than act out. The ancient adage "Know thyself" pertains to this inner exploration and development of the human potential that lies in the human soul.

In our quest for wholeness, we also encounter two other conflicting aspects of self: the true self and the false self. The *true self* is what the New Testament defines as the *kingdom within*. It is the higher self, the divine part of a human being. Everything good, noble and gentle, pleasant and generous emanates from the true self. Like unveiling a statue, once we remove distortions and superficialities, we are able to see the potential of the true self.

The *false self* consists of everything negative within a person. Haunted by compulsive desires, pained by abrupt angers, hesitant toward unrealistic ambitions, the person dominated by the false self is at enmity with joy. Its nature is to be envious, helpless, worried, critical, judgmental, unstable, in a state of perpetual dissatisfaction.

An effort to harmonize all aspects of self, an awareness of our authentic identity, will diffuse our pains and follies and will give us inner peace and personal wisdom to pursue life and living with minimum anxiety.

In your quest for self-discovery, you probably received some help from institutions: home, school, church or temple, psychotherapy, AA, Al-anon, Recovery, or other support services. Did you accept much help from your parents or peers? Or did you prefer to establish an identity separate from them? Adolescent years, as you remember them, were a period of great change in your personality.

The awareness of your identity, as brave and knowledgeable as you tried to be, unquestionably caused a great deal of concern. If you were blessed with understanding parents or a significant other who patiently explained and prepared you for life, truly you were lucky; your identity and sexuality were probably not frightening issues. Whether or not culture and education provided some understanding of this period for you, the fact remained that you were initiated into adulthood. Hormonal development, genital sensations, body changes, make-up and style of dress — all contributed to your awareness that out of the world of adolescence an adult was formed who would last a lifetime. People who are not adequately initiated into adulthood feel passive and unable to say with certainty what they want out of life. They feel lack of self-autonomy, make poor choices, feel deprived and exploited. The revolution of genders, extreme feminism or male superiority, began out of need to compensate for feelings of inferiority in femininity or masculinity. Those who were never properly initiated feel they must repeatedly prove themselves. These problems basically begin in adolescence.

During adolescent years, most young people, as they strive to fulfill their roles as mature persons, become frustrated, for our culture does not provide a milieu conducive to the fulfillment of normal biological urges. As a consequence, most people fail to find a desirable and adequate means of self-fulfillment. Some hate being women and strive to deny their femininity, forcing themselves to simulate male behavior. Others hate being men and take on female attributes. They attempt to belittle or deny their biologically assigned roles in order to avoid the frustrations that would ensue if their biological roles were fulfilled. They give their children the impression that to succumb to the temptation of being a wife and mother or husband and father is to expose themselves to slavery under an indifferent, if not cruel, master. Some women stifle their multiple potentialities by equating femininity with parasitic living. Some men succumb to feelings of despair, seeing themselves as slaves to a demanding family system. They then claim that their other potentials were actually illusions or that their talents were destined to atrophy — the price they paid for biological expression. Many men and women see themselves as martyrs to their biological and social roles, viewing their gender and its cultural demands as a cross to be borne.

For example, if your parents did not find rich and multiple gratification in their own male-female interaction, inevitably they created a struggle for you. You need to get hold of yourself and say, "I come from my mother, and I also come from my father, and without a doubt, I have some of their characteristics. I have also been influenced by them and by my environment, but now I am in charge. I can redesign and redefine my life to match my needs today." The identification with your past may lead you to an unsatisfactory distortion of your inherent human potential. It may lead to relinquishment of other drives, strengths, and good qualities, or it may lead to repression, passivity, negativism, and psychological impotence.

The truth of the matter is that the identification process for girls and boys often fails to find a desirable model in the parents. Add to the process peer and societal pressures and cultural demands, and you have a confused identity. However, our amazing survival potential often carries us through and into adulthood not irreparably traumatized.

As you explore your life, you may realize that your growth toward biological, psychological, and sociological maturity has suffered considerably. Perhaps here lies part of the void that you are experiencing today. Filling the void implies a success-ful transfer of feelings, originally directed toward the parent, to a new love object that is not taboo. Equally important, it im-plies a capacity for emotional gratification in the biologically determined role into which you were born.

An elementary step is to tell yourself: "I am who I am!" Don't just mumble it; say it vigorously. *"I am who I am!"* This is all you have, the person that you are. Let's summarize:

You have a body, but you are not your body. Your body may be in various conditions of health, it may be rested or tired, but the conditions have nothing to do with yourself. You value your body as a precious instrument of experience and of action in the outer world, but it is only an instrument. You treat your body well, you keep it in good health, but it is not yourself. You have a body, but you are not your body.

You have feelings, but you are not your feelings. Your feelings and emotions are diversified, changing, sometimes contradic-tory. They may swing from love to hate, from calm to anger, from joy to sorrow or vice versa, and yet your essence — your true self — does not change. Feelings and emotions come from you; you may monitor them and assume responsibility for them, but they do not necessarily represent your true na-ture, your soul. You can accept them, understand them, observe them, utilize and direct them harmoniously, but you are not them.

You have a mind, but you are not your mind. Your mind is a valuable tool of discovery, development, and expression, but it is not the essence of your being. Its contents are constantly changing as it embraces new ideas, knowledge, and experience. Often it refuses to obey you. Therefore, it cannot be you, your real self. It is an organ of knowledge of both the outer and inner worlds, but it is not your self. You have a mind that develops and produces ideas, but you are not your mind.

Once you comprehend that you are not your body or your mind or your feelings, you will realize that you are a self, a cen-ter of consciousness, a core of will. As such, you will be able to *observe, direct,* and *employ* all your psychological processes and your physical strengths. Initially, this challenge may sound like another language. It is. It is a language of self-development, an invitation to healthier and more productive living.

You have a desire, whatever it might be: to be wealthy, to be basking in the Caribbean sun, or to have an ideal job. But you are not your desires. Desires are aroused by drives, physical and emotional, or by various influences. They are often changeable and contradictory with alternations of attraction and repulsion. These are your desires, but you are not your desires.

You engage in various activities and play many roles in life. Sometimes willingly and sometimes unwillingly you play these roles as well as possible. You may be a son or a daughter, a mother or father, husband or wife, student or teacher, artist or executive, carpenter or builder. But all these are images, important on one level because they are roles that you are playing and can choose to play and can observe yourself playing. Therefore, you are not any of them. You are your self. You are not your image, and you are not only the actor.

Let's be a bit more specific. You feel like a victim. You have a victim's image. You feel persecuted or suffer injustice, and you perceive your reality in this light. You have some very deep and strong feelings. You feel trapped. You are aware that there is not much you can do. But there is. Think in view of what you have learned thus far. *You have a victim image,* but you are not your image. You are not this victim. Focus on this thought: you are not this victim. Although someone gave you an ugly label or you gave it to yourself, you do not have to become that label.

But what if you feel deprived, mistreated, misunderstood, empty, lonely, weak, defenseless, inadequate, scared? Finding yourself in such a state of mind, your tendency may be to pay back those who have been *unjust* to you. You may search for a cause of the feeling of emptiness and boredom, always hoping that you can fill the aching gap and free yourself from pain.

In times of doubt and conflict there is no other way to regain peace in your life except to find a way from within. Being a self is a responsibility as well as a right. External forces, significant people in your life, may insist that you stifle your self because they do not like what they see and hear. However, no one can silence or distort the real self. No matter how many times your self is repressed or broken down, something is always there within pushing forward, insisting upon expression. This inward insistence creates anxiety for a while, for the outside world demands shrewdness and control. However, the inner self is thrusting forward, requiring self-expression.

If we did not possess this unique life force, we would all be like robots — controlled, manipulated, and attuned to the rules and demands of others. We are not mechanical devices that can be activated by pushing a button, and we never will be. No matter how totally we are programmed, in the most unexpected moments our spirit will rise and make its claim upon our life.

The trap in which we are caught is our lack of understanding that we are fighting symptoms. Feelings are not reasons. In essence, the feeling of being deprived or mistreated is the memory of the old pain of self-pity that we experienced as children when our desires were frustrated. Any time we make a comparison and feel someone is getting along better than we are, we conjure up the memory of old pain.

Feeling deprived and acting like inferior, second-class passengers in life are no more than results of our failure to develop the habit of both emotional and physical self-reliance; we retain from childhood the mistaken expectation that others should clean up our messes, take care of us, emotionally and physically, and be interested in our life and responsible for our welfare.

Do you ever lay your wallet or pocketbook down and forget to keep an eye on it while you are doing something else? Do you lay down your initiative and turn it over to somebody else to exercise it for you or in your default? The answer to both questions may be simple, and yet most of our day is programmed for us by the necessity of sleeping, getting up, going to work, doing a job, going to events, church, temple, theaters, clubs, or watching television. In all such activities, the initiative is in the hands of an outside agent, and we just go along — at best, we cooperate. Most of our initiative is abdicated in daily life, and we hope that people in general are going to show the same parental warmth and eagerness to advance our welfare as our parents did, or we hoped they would, when we were children. Such expectation leads to frustration.

As adults, we may find it rewarding if we exercise our own initiative and no longer depend upon and lean on others to do what we are capable of doing for ourselves. We are born into a group of people. We grow up among people. We may find some of them benevolent and loving. But on the other side, the same coin indicates that we are born alone, we live alone, and we die alone. No human being can escape this fate. That is exactly why we have been given this initiative, this inner strength to design our life, so that we have something on which to depend.

As we mature, we discover that *reality*, like an angel with a flaming sword, confronts us and blocks the way to our paradise, our dreams. Facing life as life is, not our fantasy, causes anxiety. We have to work hard to make an adjustment. Some people, in their pursuit of *feeling good*, indulge in an addiction — liquor, drugs, gambling, promiscuity — in an effort to avoid some existential anxiety that is normal. Their whole social life is made up of others who have made the same mistake: negating their responsibility to themselves, to their families, to society. Addiction needs to be treated professionally. The potential addict may be sidetracked by fantasy: "I'm not stupid. I just want to feel good." Such people may see their fantasies as noble dreams. However, even noble dreams can be misguided and need to be confronted honestly and vigilantly.

Conformity is a way of life in which we can waive our own initiative and responsibility for creating our own happiness. The conformists lean on fate or a parent substitute. These are the perfect consumers for whatever our current culture offers; these are the targets of slick salesmanship, the victims of manipulation, and the sad objects of dependence. "Name your needs and let us take care of you. We can even tell you what you *really* need. You don't have to think or move. Anything you want will be at your doorstep for the asking." The producers of goods and their advertisers have a ready market.

It is true that our physical life has been enriched — at a price — and it has become easier, thanks to our scientific and technological progress. The part of our humanity that suffers is our soul and our emotional self. This is where our personal initiative is imperative. Before we can let go of our infantile habits and move onward to emotionally adult self-sufficiency, we must visualize our built-in potential, an awareness of our psychic qualities and energies so we can cherish our being and enjoy the world around us.

The ability to *think* and *act* independently is an inherent capacity. There is no excuse for it being defective in about 90 percent of us; it is something everyone needs, and all of us can have it if we train ourselves. No one is born with self-reliance, but nothing can stop us from achieving it, if that is what we want. It begins when we are determined to do everything we can possibly do for ourselves, emotionally, physically, and spiritually, rather than seeking someone to do it for us.

Most people find it convenient to retain the grasping, acquisitive, possessive qualities of the child throughout life. They refuse to take responsible initiative and do something worthwhile for another person or for a charitable institution. They do, however, like to receive goods. We cannot hope to meet the conditions of the outside world if we refuse to take our active part and make a personal contribution to our environment with our presence and participation. We cannot wait for outside help or even think about it, and no dependency can help us in any way to attain happiness.

Jennie, a thirty-seven-year-old nurse, came to therapy believing she was sick, unworthy, or in some way insufficient. She saw herself as the bearer of pathology from which she hoped to be relieved, or of evil forces that she must overcome. Her unhappiness was a neurosis to be cured, her personality a defect to be corrected. Although she maintained a responsible position in a hospital, she experienced herself as broken and wished to be fixed.

She did not understand that her demanding attitude and peculiar behavior had begun in childhood. They were long ago developed as the only safe strategies that could save her from the bewildering, calamitous world in which she grew up. In her adult life, the once-upon-a-time survival tactics were no longer effective. She felt helpless, failing to grasp the freedom that she possessed as a full-grown woman to take care of herself. She felt peculiar, isolated, *out of it.*

In therapy, she recognized that the problems with which she struggled were problems common to others who also struggled with them. When she had failed to grasp her place among people, her unhappiness was compounded by unbearable loneliness and self-blame.

Jennie was a victim of naive expectations. She wanted others to serve her and grant her special privileges and special exemptions. It was tragic that she could not face a problem realistically. In her daily duties, she did not follow directions. In her insecurity she manipulated other nurses into doing her job.

In looking for a world our childhood taught us to expect, a world full of loving people who will cater to our needs and shelter us from grief and pain, we are setting ourselves up for defeat. Jennie circled around and around in her unreal world, ever unaware of people's willingness to give her the kindness and affection she craved. In her own eyes, she was either too superior for them or too inferior. She was either worthy of something better than any of them could offer her, or she was repulsive and unworthy of love.

In time she began to understand that her loneliness, while extreme, was not neurotic. It was existential loneliness, the loneliness that is intrinsic to the human condition. As Herbert Holt has stated: "Every one of us is alone in our own skin, and the ultimate loneliness, the one we all learn to live with, is our mortality. It is an existential fact that we each live and die alone."

Apart from the moments of birth and death, we form connections with each other; we establish lasting relationships by giving and receiving love, validation, reassurance.

Immature individuals cannot recognize human adult love. What they are looking for is love with no strings attached, love that makes no judgments and demands nothing in return. It is a naive notion to seek unconditional love. Only divine love is absolute. In the Old Testament we discover that God's love is a gift that requires responsibilities. We must obey the Ten Commandments. In the New Testament, although love is the unconditional gift to saints and sinners alike, Jesus emphasizes adult responsibilities. We must love our neighbor as we love ourselves, turn the other cheek, and believe in him.

We often talk about a mother's unconditional and sacrificial love; yet we know too well that when children become aware of their environment, Mommy makes her claim. She wants her child to respond to her affection. As much as parents love their children, they must set standards for their behavior in order for the children to live as members of society.

In St. Paul's First Epistle to the Corinthians, chapter 13, we find a description of absolute love: "Though I speak the language of men and of angels, and have not love, I have become a sounding brass and a noisy cymbal.... Love is kind and patient; love endures all things, believes all things, forgives all things; love never fails."

Truly, this kind of love we crave as children, but as adults we all know that such love is an ideal that we can emulate, but not a reality that we can expect to attain in life. *Proper* self-love eliminates the desperate search for unconditional love from others.

As we mature, we learn that the love we give and receive is imperfect, as we are imperfect. It is comforting to know that although the love that we are able to give and receive is imperfect, it can warm us, bodily and spiritually, as no fantasized love ever can.

One of the most destructive distortions we endlessly encounter is the illusion of becoming somebody that we are not. We compete, agonize to get ahead in order to be *one up* on those around us, living a life of anguish. Like Alice in Wonderland, we need to go behind the mirror, beyond the appearance of prestigious styles and materialism, to discover *our own nature*. We need not look outside of ourselves, envying others who present a semblance of happiness. "The Kingdom of Heaven is within you," claims the great teacher of all time, Jesus of Nazareth. We cannot turn to someone else to save us. The answer to our inner void lies within our reach and in our spiritual potential.

Each of us has been given the medicine with which to cure ourselves. It would be an unjust world indeed if this were not the situation. Each of us has an intuitive feeling that we are endowed with a central core that is not ill and cannot be touched by the evils that may be tearing at the flesh. We know that somewhere inside us, beyond the external pressures, we are at peace. Our only problem is to discover what prevents us from getting to this center-of-our-being and holding on to it.

An understandable question at this point may be: *Why can I not live at this core easily? I know it must be possible.* That is the concern of this book. A human being does not have to create this core, because it is there, a gift inherent from birth: *your self, your soul.* You do not have to learn how to seek it by some arduous discipline or self-denial. What you may need is to know that mysterious factors alienate us or seem to drag us off this center, leaving a sore emptiness inside.

When we search for the truth, we must look to the self. Our motto must be: *What do I know?* And this must be pursued without hope of final answers. Establishing a rational system of answers may offer consistency, but such a system always does violence to experience.

When we turn our attention toward our self, it is not necessarily a matter of focusing on the higher aspects of our inner being, our soul. Rather it is our total life, moment to moment. We attend to everyday experiences, to sensory impressions, to descriptions of how we experience our room, our activities, our body and its functions.

In examining our own experiences and ways of reacting, we come to discover in ourselves a *master form*, a central pattern of individual personality. This could be an exciting discovery of values along the course of the intensely personal journey into the self. This is no arrogant withdrawal from our immediate environment. It is a joyful celebration of our own special self. We seek other conditions because we do not understand the use of our own, and we go out of ourselves because we do not know what it is like within.

Fortunately for all of us, male and female, God built into us our own self-healing powers, both at the physical and psychological levels. Health is our natural state of being, and it restores itself when we refrain from habits that interfere with it. Self-health, a reality, is one of the mysteries of life.

It may be difficult for you to see your potential as a birthright alive inside you if you are currently undergoing pain, or if you have a history of emotional deprivation and emptiness. It may be easier to see this quality of your soul if you look through the eyes of Walt Whitman in *Leaves of Grass* as he gazes with admiration at animals and ponders as follows.

Thoughts to Ponder

- I think I could turn and live with animals, they are so placid and self-contained;

- I stand and look at them long and long.

- They do not sweat and whine about their condition.

- They do not lie awake in the dark and weep for their sins;

- They do not spend time discussing their duty to God.

- No one is dissatisfied, not one is demented with the mania of owning things.

- Not one kneels to another, nor to his kind that lived thousands of years ago.

- Not one is responsible or industrious over the whole earth.

Chapter 2

When I Was a Child...

Most people find it convenient to retain the
grasping, acquisitive, possessive qualities of the
child throughout life.

— *Willard Beecher*

In contrast to creatures of the animal world, human beings
spend approximately the first eighteen years of life depending on adults who often continue to prop them up far more
than is necessary for their welfare. In this land of special privileges, children depend on parents and cling to them and to
other authority figures. The young are the consumers of goods
and services produced by others. They escape responsibility
by putting their own center of gravity onto others. They learn
to use positive and negative strategies to manipulate and exploit. Children are completely dependent upon their parents,
and since *caring* is essential for their existence, they do all
they can to avoid losing those who care for them. In their
efforts to do their best, parents, at this stage in their child's
life, tend to be overindulgent and overprotective. The child,
under such circumstances, cannot be allowed to move toward
independence.

In infancy, children neither know nor care about anything
but themselves. They are the center of the universe, and this
world is their concern. They want nourishment, comfort, and
love, and they depend on the parenting or benevolent adult to
provide these; otherwise they die.

Few adults are able to recollect their nightmares and frightful experiences that, according to many theorists, traumatize

them as children. Leo Tolstoi, echoing the experience of early childhood, claims: "From the child of five to myself is but a step. But from the newborn baby to the child of five is an appalling distance."

Every creature is subject to a nurturing adult whose presence makes life possible, at least for the early stages. The human symbiotic relationship is by far the most complex one, for it continues past the early stages and, at times, carries on into adulthood. "The umbilical cord has not been cut" is a common expression in our everyday language. It denotes the fact that someone who should be an adult emotionally depends upon one or both parents.

During the first few weeks of postnatal life, human infants are unable to distinguish between themselves and their mother. Like daydreaming adults, infants cherish a magic world of kaleidoscopic imagery that is very appropriate for this age, for it protects them from having to recognize their actual helplessness. Whenever infants are moved around, turned over, bathed, diapered, or taken out of doors, they perceive the endless variety of experiences as things that happen around them. As they mature a little more, the mother continues to introduce more experiences until the child is, to a certain degree, independent.

The big moments in infants' lives are when someone feeds or fondles them. At a very early age they discover that crying brings adults to serve them when they are hungry, wet, or bored. They also find that smiling holds the attention of the adults who have the power to bring them benefits. They smile when they are picked up and cry when they are laid down. Here lies the root of manipulation; we learn how to get people to fulfill our needs. It is one of the most important survival skills we learn early in life.

The only attitude possible in the earliest stage of human life is egocentric. Infants want what they want, and they want it now. Otherwise, they display their rage. It is interesting to note that adults, too, frequently exhibit this sort of attitude, unrealistic as it may be. All children have a legitimate narcissistic need to be noticed, understood, accepted, taken seriously, and respected by their mothers or mothering adults. In the first months of life, children need to have their mother at their disposal; they must be able to use her, and to be mirrored by her.

Lucky is the child who grows up with a loving, mirroring

mother who allows herself *to be made use of* as a function of the child's narcissistic development, who allows herself to be physically and emotionally available to her child. But even a mother who is not especially warmhearted can make this development possible if she only refrains from preventing it. This enables the child to acquire from other significant adults what the mother lacks. A healthy child can make use of the smallest affective *nourishment* to be found in the immediate environment.

What about the children who lose their mothers at infancy or for whatever reason grow up without a mother? Those children will forever feel a gap, and they will seek to fulfill infantile needs from other sources such as a loving grandmother or a benevolent adult who shows understanding. Eventually such children will have to develop their own resources and make possible for themselves a better life and not depend on others to supply it; or they may choose a significant other to validate their presence and to support their transition into the adult world.

"Where do I fit in?" you may ask. At any waking moment, your thoughts, feelings, and behaviors are determined by the sum of your learning experiences since your birth. To answer the above question, to arrive at some definition of who you are, you may have to explore the development of your identity and personhood.

As a child you entered the world in a situation of great inequality. At birth you were completely helpless. Your survival depended on the experiences, instructions, and behavior of your caretakers, usually your parents or significant parental adults. Regardless of how deprived or emotionally abused you feel as an adult, you received some care in your early childhood, or you would have died. In addition to providing the food, shelter, clothing, and love needed for your physical and emotional survival, your parents were responsible for the early conditionings and images that formulated your world. You developed an understanding of the world around you through your senses.

At the present point in your existence, you are aware that you want harmony in your life. It is our human condition to want to make sense of the world. As children we wanted the same thing — to understand the world around us — and we made up what we did not understand. Since communication is dysfunctional in most families, children will distort information in order to understand. Fantasy fills in the areas where reality does not fit. Later, as we grow into adulthood, the conscious and unconscious memories of childhood become an interesting blend of truth and illusion. As children, we see with perfect clarity, but we lack judgment. It is the adult mind that creates distortions.

Have you ever caught yourself in a situation where you felt comfortable using a child's solution to an adult problem? That child still lingers on into your adult life. Observe it and value it, but be careful that it does not make adult decisions.

Your experiences began to be formulated in the cradle, and most of the coping mechanisms that deal with stress began to develop in early childhood. For example, if you experienced abandonment during the first months of your life — your mother disappeared into the kitchen to prepare your formula or went to work — today you are likely to have a difficult time forming close, intimate relationships with others, unless more favorable discoveries have replaced the early experiences. *How* you were received in your environment as a child contributed to your feelings of worthiness or unworthiness.

One day, seeing your father angry or your mother frowning, you asked, "What's wrong?" Your mother, who may have followed the "I must always be happy" rule, responded, "Nothing, dear, I am feeling just fine." To conceal her true feelings from you — the intolerable conflict between what she felt in her own psyche and what she should be feeling as a mother — she momentarily turned her back on you. You, as a child, observing your mother's movements, came up with many interpretations. You had no choice but to assume that your mother's frown had to do with you. The acute awareness of a child includes this possibility: "I'm the cause of my parent's happiness or unhappiness."

Most parents are not aware of their incongruent messages. Some think they should shield their children from negative messages for fear that they might hurt them. Actually, negative messages in many instances, even if they are straight messages of rejection of the child, may be less detrimental to the child's mental health than are the mixed messages that a child is unable to figure out. Think of a child who hears Mother saying to a friend, "I just don't like my mother. I hate her." Then the grandmother visits, and on her arrival, the mother says to the child, "Give Grandma a kiss." The child is truly confused: How can she say she hates Grandma and now asks me to kiss the object of her hate?

Most of what children learn, and all they learn in the first few months of life, is learned not from words but from voice, touch, and looks. If your mother or father spoke to you directly and allowed you to speak directly to them, the chances are that you felt validated as a person and felt important being their child. If your parents ignored your presence, if you spoke to them and they did not pay attention to what you were saying, most likely you felt excluded or rejected and developed low self-esteem, setting yourself up for a life of frustrations.

If you were an only child, and the sun rose and set upon you daily, you may have received a great deal of attention, not necessarily all positive attention, but nonetheless a rounded support from your parents. The drawback of being an only child can be a demanding attitude on the part of the parents: "This is our only hope and aspiration; this child has to fulfill all our wishes." Consequently, they develop a list of expectations; they become overprotective, sensitive, overly strict or too permissive.

If you were blessed with siblings in your family, with proper parental guidance you were able to grow side by side with brothers and sisters and, in spite of the rivalry, find your own development. If parents make the mistake of ignoring the early signs of jealous rivalry or interfering unjustly in favor of one, then their children can become so entangled in competition as to be emotionally crippled for the rest of their lives unless some intensive re-education halts the crippling.

The period of childhood serves the needs of children, but it spells disaster if, after physical maturity is reached, we continue to make infantile demands. Mature adults no longer rely on free service. They neither depend on promises nor trust experiences of others as their guide. Step by step they learn to trust themselves and rely on their own experiences to direct them.

A human being is a complex entity, but in one respect the human response is uniform. Physiologically and psychologically it is designed to avoid destructive extremes. Every response has its counterresponse. When a healthy body experiences an outpouring of adrenaline in response to rage or fear, a countermechanism also goes into action, holding the patterns of glandular and nervous response within safe limits for the organism.

You may have heard of the "fight or flight" phenomenon. This is a reaction that sends a rush of adrenaline into your system when you are confronted with danger. When confronted by a threat or a situation that we perceive as dangerous, our nervous and glandular systems become activated, resulting in faster heartbeat, muscular contraction, and more rapid breathing that prepares us to fight — or to flee if we think our enemy is too strong. The change in physiology caused by the fight-or-flight response puts stress on both body and psyche, making us feel tense and anxious. If the emergency situation does not dissipate within a short time, the added stress becomes a health hazard.

In prehistoric times, this adrenaline rush meant daily survival. Without its stimulus a Neanderthal in the path of an angry tiger or a poisonous snake would never have been able to escape. Today, in most situations, that surge of adrenaline has nowhere to go. When we are confronted with a stressful, traumatic event, the rush of adrenaline becomes an uninvited guest. We cannot very well pummel the boss who has insulted us, nor can we smash our car as we wait in traffic that is backed up for miles. Instead, we have an anxious feeling that has no outlet, a jumpiness that needs release. This situation invites the following important question: Can you bear a bit of anxiety without panic? It might be difficult to answer, but it may well provide an opportunity to explore your strengths and vulnerabilities. Living in a world of reality causes anxiety. This sort of existential anxiety can be a motive to seek a new direction in your life.

The responses of our senses have their limits. The sense of smell is particularly quick in reaching the fatigue level. When you enter a restaurant, your nose may be delighted by the savory odor escaping from the kitchen, but within a few minutes you can no longer detect the smell. You may also have noticed that although you enjoy delicious food, once the stomach is full, the food becomes a bore. Beautiful music, when heard too often, becomes an annoyance. As limited human beings, we have responses to life that are limited. Simply stated, we cannot be in a state of ecstasy very long; we cannot have an ongoing orgasm! The very thought is torture.

Institutions and society add their own limits to our opportunities for ecstasy. Our jobs are not as rewarding as we would like; our families restrict our enjoyments; our interaction with bankers, builders, electricians, and plumbers provoke anxiety. Our daily life tends to be as imperfect as we are. Mass media try to seduce us with promises and to fill our emptiness with fantasy, causing us further dissatisfaction. Numerous aspects of our civilization conspire to keep us on the path to fantasyland; for example, most of us mistakenly depend upon material possessions for our happiness, as if we were children in toyland unable to find the toy we want.

At times we have high expectations of others. We want them to respond to our needs, take care of us, or accept our advice. St. Paul summarizes our human predicament of growing up:

> When I was a child, I talked like a child, I thought like a child, I reasoned like a child. When I became a man, I put childish ways behind me.

Is that a possibility for you — to put childish ways behind you? If your answer is yes, you may consider the following.

- Pause for a precious moment.

- Close your eyes.

- Take three deep breaths.

- Relax.

- Using your own name, ask yourself, "[Your name], who are you?"

- Gently and benevolently describe yourself.

Stop here and write a long paragraph that tells the truth about you. Remember, the way you perceive your individual self will formulate the definition of who you are.

Now read over this definition and revise it if you wish to come closer to the real you.

Once the definition of yourself is complete, stop and think carefully. Ask: "Is this really me, or is it what others have said about me?" The self-image of any person is a product designed by parents, relatives, teachers, peers, and a number of external influences such as culture, environment, and circumstances.

In your efforts to define your life, you may have to transcend the image that others have formulated for you and begin with the basics.

If you have a notion that you are no good, weak, or worthless, and you find yourself defective, unconsciously you will seek people to confirm this identity.

If you see yourself as a person with adult aspirations, not mired down in childish concerns, you will recognize qualities in yourself that can help you attain the desired goals in your life.

As adults, we may choose to "put away childish things," magic thinking, mental and physical habits that perpetuate childish dependence upon other things and other people. However, as we consciously bring our childhood to an end, fear of using our own initiative and bearing responsibility may threaten us, and we may feel blocked emotionally with regard to how we are going to enter this unknown arena of the world ahead of us. Each of us faces the fork in the road, and there is seldom anyone to guide us.

In ancient times there was a mentor, a tutor, a sort of benevolent teacher assigned the task of piloting the young person from puberty into adulthood.

Throughout history, parents have loved their children, cared for them more or less tenderly at all times and in all societies, but they have not always devoted themselves totally to their children's happiness. At one time the upper class relegated their responsibilities to wet-nurses, nannies, au pair help, governesses, and boarding schools. The working class put their children out as apprentices. The very poor sent their children out to beg or steal, sold them into slavery or prostitution, and did whatever they had to do in order to survive.

In recent history, specifically since the Second World War, parents have made enormous sacrifices to give their children whatever they desire, whatever the parents themselves as children did not have. Parents often feel guilty over every mistake they make in feeding, caring, and toilet-training, and they are afraid to impose discipline or punishment. The consequences of our child-centered society are now being felt. Our generation continues to look for the source of its miseries in the sins of its parents, sins of both commission and omission. A new society has been formed, that of the wounded children. These prisoners of the past seek a new form of therapy to regress into their early childhood to find that wounded child. The hope is that they will be able to cure the inner child and help it to grow benevolently into adulthood. Who can say that such a therapy is not helpful, at least to a portion of its followers?

A great deal can be said about those who indulge in narcissistic rage — blaming their current condition on the wounds inflicted upon them in early childhood and wishing things could have been different. In a state of passivity, they complain that the world stinks. Perhaps they have a point. Life is not perfect — but neither does it stink. How each of us adjusts to it is a personal choice and responsibility. By continuing to blame our wounds on the past we immobilize ourselves in the present; we stop living. But, if we invest time and energy to change those parts of our life that can be changed on an emotional, cognitive, physical, or spiritual level, we stand a better chance of being rewarded.

Life is life. This is all we have. I did not make it this way. You did not make it this way. We can make it better if we assume some responsibility, primarily, if we develop an attitude of caring about the quality of life we live daily.

Of course there is a vast number of people who feel deprived, accustomed to the cloud of discontent hanging over them, even though things may be going well for them. They feel wounded and lack joy in what they are doing. As they contemplate the nature of their problem, they are at a loss to point to any particular thing that they can blame for their unhappiness.

Debbie, a thirty-two-year-old married woman with a five-year-old child and a hard-working husband who, she claimed, loved them both, came to my office after nine years of consistent therapy. She was a veteran of religious retreats, sensitivity marathons, scream therapy, touch-and-feel, biofeedback, hypnotherapy, astrology, and modern psychoanalytical therapy.

Upon the recommendation of her pastor, she decided to see me, in full anticipation that there must be something I could do. She survived three sessions with me, which gave her sufficient time to discover that I did not operate a beauty salon or a health spa where she could have her psyche shampooed, touched up, teased, or primped. I was not the imagined surgeon who could painlessly remove the mole, the wart, the single unfortunate personality trait with a magic psychological scalpel.

Disappointed that I could promise no cure for her discontent, no Garden of Eden without a serpent, she decided to seek a different course, a more charismatic therapist.

Debbie invested precious time, energy, and money seeking solutions from external resources. Nothing wrong with that. Authorities may provide direction, but they cannot provide magic solutions to life's problems. Perhaps it was difficult for Debbie to delve into herself and face the existential agony of being alive, to tolerate the temporary discomfort of feeling empty within. Could she appreciate her womanhood, her sensitivity to life, and her unique qualities of loving and caring? Could she focus on her immediate environment, her child and her husband, and respond to their needs even for a while? Of course she could, but in her preoccupation for an *ideal* solution, she negated her responsibility.

After seventeen years of psychoanalytical therapy thirty-seven-year-old Dr. H. came to me seeking a permanent cure for his boredom. In a heart-to-heart talk, I reassured him that his boredom was not a sickness. Boredom is an inevitable part of the human condition. Dr. H. had learned long ago to keep busy. Endowed with superior intelligence for invention and creation, he had removed himself from the real world and confined himself to his work in a windowless laboratory, the basement under his office. This was a mixed blessing; the more he indulged in his anticipated invention, the more he removed himself from ordinary life. Gradually, even working for a living was boring.

Dr. H. tolerated boredom for a while. Then he discovered that when we cut ourselves off from genuine interaction with others, we cut off the largest part of ourselves.

A month after our first encounter, Dr. H. reported to me that a friend had invited him to see his orchard. He went to pick apples and to chat, and for the first time in many years he enjoyed himself. He even brought me half a dozen.

Six months later, Dr. H. bought himself a twenty-four-foot boat; he learned how to sail and now spends many leisure hours off the Jersey coast. He no longer speaks of boredom. His practice as an oral surgeon is blossoming and he talks about it with excitement. He met a beautiful woman with whom he fell in love; they are now married.

Magic cure? Absolutely not. Magic only makes people blind and deaf to reality. Magic therapy offers a weekend or a week in ecstasy: being free, uninhibited, and unafraid of releasing the demoniac desires and impulses that most of us believe that we have repressed within us — without having to face the social consequences. Dr. H. came to realize that magic is a dangerous substitute for reality. In connecting with some real people, in all their diversity and uniqueness, he discovered his real self. Above all, he took charge of living his life rather than wasting his substance in dreaming about it.

Innumerable case histories describing human ambiguities and aberrations could be related, but such an approach would hardly be of benefit to anyone, for no two cases are alike. A human psyche is not an automobile that a skillful mechanic could repair and return in top condition to the owner. The human psyche is a unique product of inheritance and environment, developed through a long maturing process during which it learns its own identity as separate from that of parents, siblings, and friends. To assume that this complex and unique entity, a human being, can be taken into a shop, office, clinic, or laboratory for quick therapy is naive.

The source of most emotional problems lies in a state of persisting infantilism, which is a refusal on the part of the individual to give up childhood habits. An adult is expected to become a beneficial presence in society, to produce goods and services and to give products in exchange for those of others. Children are passive-receptive. As they get older, they have to give up their "getting" style of life and become active, productive members of their community. They have to put away childish things.

Is there something we can learn from children? We can emulate their spontaneity, creativity, and joy. In their innocence, they trust what they do, they get involved in activities, and they know what makes them happy.

Thoughts to Ponder

- The danger of trying to recapture a lost childhood is that you may succeed.

- Some adults are children with wrinkles.

- Some adults take a lifetime to get over their childhood.

- Who ever said that the purpose of parenthood is to make children happy?

- There is a price for every attainment in life. How much are you prepared to pay for your attainments?

- If we can work a little on ourselves every day, we will gradually gain a great deal.

- There is a dynamic, a spiritual strength, in each human that vivifies our growth, and if we ignore its purpose, we do so at our peril.

Chapter 3

Now That I Am an Adult...

The ability to *think* and *act* independently is an inherent capacity.

—*Herbert Holt*

You have begun an important task: making a transition from childhood to adulthood. At some point you may face the loneliness attached to all beginnings. You may still be carrying mental or physical habits, remnants of childhood, that keep you dependent and immature.

As you look around you, at people you know well or others who surround you daily, you will be tempted to raise the question: Why is it so rare to see human beings who can stand on their own feet? Such a question goes right to the heart of the human condition. We are all dependent. No human stands alone. The unspoken implication is that the degree of our dependency dictates our happiness or our unhappiness.

There is a healthy dependency between friends who reciprocally do good things for each other. This may be seen in the healthy dependency that exists between marital partners. On a larger scale, there is the unavoidable dependency we have on our government, on the armed forces and police departments to protect us, on hospitals and institutions for our health, on churches and temples for our spiritual welfare, on our school systems for the education of our young, and on the producers of goods. A long list can be compiled of instances of a sort of indispensable interdependency among nations, institutions, and people, which benefits the common welfare.

Unhealthy dependency is noticeable when a person in either

thought or behavior, overtly or covertly, implores: "Please, someone look after me." Such a person suffers from chronic "soseme-mania," a term I coined meaning "a passion to be saved by another." Such people can hardly bear even imagining what it would be like to recognize that they are in charge of their own lives. They would feel let down, exploited, even betrayed.

Completing the fifth year of recovery after a devastating divorce, Loretta, in her early fifties, made a wish: "I wish I could find someone who knows the true meaning of life, someone who would love me for the person that I am, someone who would take good care of me, a good man I could depend upon to look after me. Then I would be happy."

I listened to Loretta's naive notion, and with a sympathetic smile, I said, "A magic man! A caretaker is not difficult to find. But how are you going to feel in his domain?"

After a moment's reflection, she said, "I would probably grow to hate him, or I'd want to punish him because I'd find myself dependent upon him."

One of the realities of life is that all our meanings are built into us from the outside, from our interaction with others. Our whole world of right and wrong, good and bad, our name, precisely who we are: all are grafted onto us. We feel insecure about offering things on our own. How can we, if we do not get an external authority to approve of us? Since our birth, we feel indebted or even controlled by others — parents or parental adults, teachers, peers, or authority figures. Here lies an inherent fear: What if others disapprove of us or even do not like us? The thought holds us back and stifles our initiative.

As you are entering the adult world, it is normal to feel scared or intimidated by the massive impact of societal expectations. Standing agape in front of the biblical whale, we are afraid we may end up like Jonah. Will I be able to make it in this chaotic world, or will I die? Will I find joy or misery in this life? It is understandable that you may find yourself reluctant to move out into the overwhelming world, into the dangers that lurk in the corners. You may shrink back from losing yourself in the all-consuming appetites of others, from spinning out of control in the clutchings and clawings of people, beasts, and machines.

Mass media conspire to unleash the furies, making life a

nightmare: decline in the national economy, unemployment, crime, war, natural disasters, international unrest. News of such events can suck us up, sap our energies, submerge us, take away our self-control, give us exposure to so much experience so quickly that we burst, make us stick out among others, lure us onto dangerous ground, load us up with new responsibilities that need enormous strength to bear, expose us to new contingencies, new chances. Despite the negativity that surrounds us, what can keep our head above the water is the knowledge that we are here because many who came before us met the challenges of their day. The awareness that some good things are also happening is encouraging. Think of *something* good. At least you are alive, and that is important.

Of course nothing happens without a beginning. All of life and all realities, except the absolute reality, God, begin somewhere, somehow, sometime. The pain of every beginning is the pain of birth into a new dimension of life. It cannot be shared at its deepest level, for it touches the very core of the human spirit, the soul.

Beginnings have a simple beauty and excitement about them. Whenever we start anew, we share in the innocence of childhood and the wisdom of maturity. Only the wise and innocent are willing to begin again. To be ourselves, to be genuine, to be authentic and true, to be worthy of life, we must begin.

The beginner is, at best, awkward, scared. If you are just beginning a new direction in life, understandably you will be eager, yet hesitant, authentic, yet fearful. Currently, you may be experiencing conflicting moods, or this book may be triggering new thoughts. "Can I really learn something beneficial from this reading?" Raising a question like this, you may find yourself in a state of aloneness that is far more encompassing than the aloneness that springs from an absence of people. It is an effort with your own self. To begin a new direction in your life, you must begin.

Writing about a new beginning, or discussing the topic of self-restoration in a workshop setting, or exploring the human potential in a therapy session is easy. One feels elated and supported in Al-anon or Alcoholics Anonymous meetings. They are most effective. In the presence of a good speaker or a wise counselor, the person in pain finds relief. Where you are in the real world is different. You wake up in the morning and you have that dreadful feeling as you ask yourself: "What's in store for me today?" You recoil from the uneasiness that you are not totally in control of your destiny. You either go back to bed or linger on, thinking that you need a cup of coffee or a cigarette to help you face the day.

Fully awake, you now think of certain tasks you have to do, but you sense a resistance. You find the uncertainties of life hard to accept; the wrongs of society upset you; your own current situation causes anxiety and sometimes downright depression. When you hear about unemployment, accidents, crime, and war... when your best friend's brother is dying of AIDS... when the plane you were to take is hijacked... when your mate decides to leave you for another... when the person you are in love with has developed cancer — the list can go on and on. You can be mad as hell and refuse to take it anymore, but that will not stop the pain. To shake off the anxious feelings, many people resort to magical devices that provide temporary illusions of control. Some take a drink, others use drugs, and others seek whatever therapeutic experiences happen to be in vogue.

Many people try to develop a philosophy for living in the present. Such an approach to life and living cannot be designed by a professional. It has to be developed by each individual according to that individual's emerging needs. Professionals in the healing arts provide a climate conducive to growth. In a therapeutic session, individuals have an opportunity to explore the possible changes that are needed in their lives, and they must decide which change is a priority. Self-help books provide guidelines to life's dilemmas, which you may find beneficial. However, regardless of how valid and valuable these external offers are, it is the individual's choice to develop viable options. No external authority can provide you with a philosophy for living. Anyone who assumes such authority over your life usurps your own initiative. Ultimately, you will resent living a life that you did not create. Here is your current challenge: to design and redesign your mode for living.

Burt, a tall, handsome twenty-nine-year-old man, came into my office, complaining about the unfairness of life. He seemed hopeless. He took over the session, ranting about his parents, his peers, the social system, his insensitive boss, his job, the lack of good jobs in the market. When his repertoire was complete and he had linked all the injustices into a chain of personal misery, he resorted, with paranoid persistence, to an attack on generalized targets: the state, the federal government, the politicians, and so on. These grievances were against a world that refused to give him the large share of goodies that he felt he deserved.

The trouble with Burt was that all the rational controls he had developed in the previous twenty years had been shattered, and he was left with a feeling of rage. Rage turned into destructive patterns that nearly cost him his life. His uncontrolled emotions cut him off from the relationships that had sustained him, challenged him, kept him alive and human. It took a long time to recruit his intellectual faculties and help him separate from his instant rages and eventually guide him to the realization that feelings, although a rich part of our humanity, are not the whole self. Feelings need to be understood as personal property, not always useful. Of course, feelings cannot be ignored as unimportant or childish. In therapeutic settings, getting in touch with one's feelings so they can be understood and appropriated is very important. Being in charge of our feelings and emotions is a sign of maturity. When feelings are not guided by logic and are left to run rampant, they can destroy everything of value in an individual's life.

All situations are not as severe as Burt's; fortunately, he found significant improvement with professional help. I believe that he could not have done it alone. That is my opinion. But who can question the human potential? Had Burt been left alone, would he, instinctively, as do the shipwrecked, have looked around for some saving grace, something to cling to? Since his survival was at stake, would he not have attempted to bring a sort of order into the chaos of his life? I do not know.

At times, people like Burt, who hit the bottom of despair and are emotionally destroyed, somehow self-transcend and make a new beginning. Their self begins to relate to powers beyond therapeutic interventions. The self employs its own uniqueness, its own power, which organizes external realities and harmonizes them to match the inner needs. The person matures physically, emotionally, and intellectually.

Human beings are able to think, and we can think in abstractions — beauty, logic, justice. We can think about the past, the present, and the future. This capacity of awareness enables us to see ourselves as others see us and to have feelings for others.

Whatever thoughts we develop about others dictate our feelings toward them. The gift of thought comes at a high price,
the price of anxiety and inner discomfort. Awareness of self is
no simple and easy matter. Children face the frightful prospect
of being out on their own, alone, without the full protection of
their parents. It is no wonder that when they begin to perceive
themselves as separate beings they may feel terribly powerless
in comparison with the great and strong adults around them.

Children who are blessed with healthy and supportive parents will proceed in their development despite the anxiety
caused by being left alone for a while and the worry of con-
tending with a possible crisis. Yet children with loving and
caring parents will, nevertheless, face anxiety, growing pains,
because of their *smallness*. At times it is only natural that they
will misunderstand even the best intentions of their parents.

Children who are caught in the web of troubled parents and
are constantly exposed to quarrels, fights, and violence will have
a hard time adjusting emotionally to life in later years. They will
feel insecure and rejected, doubting their presence as persons in
an adult world. For survival purposes, they might even manipulate their environment, cling to their parents or other adults
in search of a *self* that they can claim as their own. Nearly all
adults are still searching on the long journey of life to achieve
selfhood on the basis of their early childhood experiences.

The self always grows in interpersonal relationships. In our
world of conformity, where society expects us to fit the mold
if we are to be accepted, a human being suffers immensely to
establish a self that is genuine and authentic. There is a struggle to maintain one's uniqueness, to transcend the temptation
of becoming someone else.

"I think, therefore I am," said the French philosopher, imply-
ing that we exist as a self because we are thinking creatures. We
could expand on the idea by saying, "I feel, therefore I am." Is
this enough to define the self? Besides thinking and feeling, the
list of functions of self can be enriched according to our perceptions. Any attempt to define the self would only limit this
inner reality, no matter what we name it — self, psyche, soul,
spirit, identity. For our purposes, let's describe the self as the
"harmonizer."

Visualize an orchestra made up of many instruments and
players. One person stands in front and conducts, making ab-

solutely sure that each player is reading the notes correctly to produce harmony. The self is the conductor, the harmonizing function within the individual, the means by which one human being can relate to another. The self is not the instruments, nor is it the sum of the melody or cacophony that they produce. The self is the capacity that enables one to conduct the orchestra. It is the core from which one sees, hears, and is aware of the different movements of living.

This limited definition of self introduces the possibility that we are thinking, feeling, intuitive, and acting entities. However, our development as humans is neither simple nor automatic. Like a tree, we grow on all sides according to the tendencies of the inward forces that make us living things, according to the environmental contributions, and gradually we fulfill our potentialities only as we consciously plan and choose.

In contrast to the condition of the tree or of the animal, which must fend for itself within a few weeks of birth, human beings go through infancy and childhood in the difficult task of maturation. Gradually, individuals acquire knowledge, skills, and inner strength that enable them to choose and decide which direction they need to take at a given moment. Joy is the effect that comes when our self begins to function unhindered. Joy, rather than happiness, is the goal of life, for joy is the feeling that accompanies our fulfilling of our natures as human beings. As we experience our own true self, we become more alive. In this stage, we see our errors, make allowances for our prejudices, use guilt feelings and anxiety as experiences to learn from, and make decisions with a greater sense of responsibility. This is a healthy self.

It is an undisputed reality that your past experiences, from your earliest childhood until today, cannot be changed. Regardless of how beneficial or traumatic they were, unlike a movie or a book, they cannot be edited or erased. However, from this moment on, your attitude and disposition about your past can be different. Your highest quality at this reading is yourself, the awareness and acceptance of who you are. Here lies your ability to distinguish between you, *the person* that you are, and the world. This process can only be a *rebirth* that embraces a new and broader meaning, an awakening into a new strength that you can employ.

You may feel the pull back: "I'm not ready for this. This is not for me." Understandably, you hesitate, and you may want to close the book. This would be another way to evade the challenge of personal growth. All of us fear growth because it means abandoning the familiar for the unknown. It involves risks. Andras Angyal says it well:

> Abandoning the familiar for the unknown always involves risks. When the changes are far-reaching or precipitous they are bound to arouse anxiety. The view that growth is inseparable from anxiety is shared by practically all thinkers who have substantially contributed to our understanding of anxiety.... The anxiety felt at the prospect of dissolution of one's current mode of being has been related by some to the fear of final dissolution.... Since growth requires that old patterns die, willingness "to die" is a precondition of living.... Excessive fear of death is often a correlate of the neurotic fear of growth and change.

Suppose you agree to do a friend a favor, but suddenly you change your mind. "I don't feel like it," you may say. Why? Maybe you are afraid that you will not know where to start or where to draw the line and that you will find yourself being used and exploited by your friend — if you give him an inch, he may take a mile. Somehow we lack the stable sense of self that would permit us to have our *yes* and our *no* in such situations. This fear is also related to the fact that as a part of the pattern of modern life we know too many people too superficially and we experience too little responsibility for each other.

Every human being possesses strengths and weaknesses, and if you feel good about whatever strengths you possess — for instance, you know yourself to be a caring person — you will not seek constant reassurance from others. But if your personality consists of only negative qualities — "I'm short"; "I'm fat"; "I'm ugly"; "I'm jealous"; "I'm ignorant"; "I'm stupid"; "I can't do anything right" — if this is all you are, and I have a hard time believing that, then I suggest that you become *vigilant*. In the process of redefining yourself, you may have to make some appropriate choices, not to hurt yourself further and not to hurt others. Like an artist, take time to put the best colors upon the new portrait of yourself. You need not follow the majority. Listen to your inner voice: What is it that your rediscovered self wants or needs?

As you are reading, look through your window and visualize a beautiful oak tree. If you needed wood for your fireplace, you could cut it down and chop it into small logs so that you would have a winter's supply of firewood. If you needed a cabin, a skillful carpenter could convert the tree into useful planks. If you wanted a chest of drawers, what would you do? In a painstaking effort, a furniture-maker would employ all kinds of special tools to carve out your desired design. The potential is in the tree; it takes sensory organs, time, energy, and a creative eye to bring out the potential of the tree.

The illustration speaks to us about our abilities and the possibilities ahead of us. In your search for a genuine, adult identity that speaks to you exclusively, you may start working to produce a self that is joyful and productive, a personality that is forthright, honest, loving, fearless, and caring. We are, according to the Bible, created in God's image and likeness. Surely that is a possibility worth exploring.

To become more fully human, more fully alive, the first step is necessary: you need to be in touch with your life force, your harmonized self, and be willing to take whatever risks are necessary for change to occur. The process of change necessitates the willingness and ability to acquire new awareness at a cognitive, emotional level, as well as at a visionary and intentional level. Your creative eye has to visualize the personality that you are seeking to develop.

Genetically, you were endowed with feelings, thoughts, and behaviors that were gradually enhanced by additional experiences. You can be proud of patterns of living that have been productive for you. However, you need to be careful of the negative aspects of your life lest they cause damage in your transition. You need not focus on the extinction of bad habits. The change that you are seeking, the visualization of the *newness* in you, will transform the bad habits. The moment you begin to use new ways to make your life more joyful, the old ways will die of disuse.

Of course, discovering new ways to deal with your daily life will not always be pleasant. There may be times when you will feel discouraged and in despair. A principal thought to keep in mind is that you are different from others who are exposed to new experiences. As such, try to be respectful and attentive to your individual needs. See and select what fits your personality; reject experiences that you find inappropriate for yourself. Remember, essentially the learning process is a discovery or, more accurately, a rediscovery of knowledge that is already within yourself. Truly, you will feel great excitement when you get in touch with something you knew all along but did not know you knew.

Thoughts to Ponder

- Take a gentle and honest look at yourself. What qualities do you like about the person that you are? Describe them on a piece of paper, pointing out in what ways these qualities make your life happier and more productive.

- What are the qualities that you do not like about yourself? Describe them briefly, listing areas where these qualities prevent your progress.

- How do the negative qualities of your father and mother express themselves in you? Have their flaws become your flaws? Can you think of one good quality that you inherited from your parents?

- Do you ever feel that you are like your mother or like your father, or do you feel you are a composite of both? Are you ever an individual of your own kind?

- Do you find that in your daily functions you are under the influence of your parents or other significant adults of your early childhood? Can you abandon your past programming?

- Do you ever wonder why you exhibit the patterns and traits that you dislike in your parents? Can you leave them behind you?

- When you stop confusing your self-definition with the definition your parents have of you, you have attained uniqueness.

Chapter 4

The Twin Within

The single relationship that is truly central and
crucial in a life is the relationship to self.

—*Jo Courdet*

Many years ago I saw a Russian ballet performance at the Rose
Bowl Theater in Los Angeles. The act that stole the show and
got a standing ovation was the wrestling of identical twin boys.
Most skillfully they threw each other down, climbed on a table,
fell to the floor and got up again; the match continued and cap-
tivated the audience, which applauded appreciatively. The act
ended when the twins uncovered themselves to reveal the per-
former, one person. Ingeniously, the actor had managed to fold
himself into two parts, each dressed in identical clothing; one
part physically wrestled with the other.

I often recall the wrestling twins when one of my clients
makes a statement such as: "Sometimes I think I am two
people," or "There is a part of me that fights the other," or
"There is a part of myself I don't like." It seems that most of us
have a twin within, who constantly wrestles, resents, and resists
the other. This inner fight or match causes discomfort, makes
life difficult, limits choices, stifles our potential, and results in
a life of discontent.

Let us assume that we all enter life with a basic concept of
self. When we are loved, the self feels fulfilled. When our presence is appreciated and validated by significant others, a good
feeling, an aura of wellness, permeates the inner self. Individuals who focus totally on this good part of their personality
not only exalt themselves but are bound to look at their actual

self — all that they are at a given time, body and spirit with healthy and unhealthy qualities. The exalted or idealized self becomes not only the twin to be pursued, but also a measuring device with which we measure our real self, including the other, vulnerable twin.

Have you ever wrestled with the twin emotions of desire and fear that surround human sexuality? Desire drives you toward a legitimate way to express, enjoy, and appreciate your sexuality. Fear drives you toward a legitimate way to control, bridle, or repress so dangerous a force. Sexual mores have always sought to move creatively between desire and fear. The goodness of the desire must be affirmed and respected or we deny the essential goodness of God's creation. The reality of the fear creates the necessary controls so that a constructive expression of human sexuality can be achieved. Sex is powerful and touches life at its very depths, but it is more than physical thrills. It is an emotional, a psychological, and even a spiritual experience.

Fear, the other half of the twins, serves to remind us that we cannot separate sex and love without painful consequences. No one can use another person without turning that person into a thing. No one wants to be manipulated, fed a line, made a conquest. Yet there are times when a part from within succumbs to the temptation to exploit another human being.

In focusing on a less desirable part of the self, we tend to dislike it or even hate it. We like the part that performs well and receives admiration, but when our limitations or human frailties hinder a *perfect* performance, we become angry or disturbed with ourselves. The fact remains that we are still one person, however divided into two people — the ideal person and the countertwin who is always interfering, always disturbing. Whether we eat, sleep, work, play, or make love, that twin is there. We think that things could be different, better, if we only had another occupation, lived in another country, moved to another house, took a trip, or divorced our mate and married another one. But reality knocks at the door of our self, telling us that we are limited human beings endowed with limited time, energy, power, and endurance, and we cannot really get everything that we want out of life.

If we indulge in grandiosity to impress the world around us, performance becomes awkward, the fight of the twins shakes us within, and the unique lover may suddenly be impotent. We are at war with ourselves. This civil war is not directed so much against the ugly part of self as against the healthy part. It is an inner conflict, hindering our potential. However, maturity strengthens our ability to tolerate ambiguity and the civil war that rages within. This conflict may bring balance and moderation into our lives. It is a natural, central mechanism that can create order and harmony.

Harold illustrates the point well. He was a thirty-seven-year-old tall, handsome, intelligent teacher who sought therapy because he believed he was sick, unworthy, and inadequate. He perceived himself as a bearer of pathology from which he hoped to be relieved. From the age of sixteen, he felt dissatisfied with life. Some twenty years of chronic unhappiness, which eventually disguised itself as a stomach ulcer, had to be cured, his defective personality had to be corrected. He experienced himself as divided and wished to be restored — a noble expectation and a serious task.

Although he was highly intelligent, Harold had a hard time understanding that his *crazy* attitude and destructive behavior had begun in childhood. As a helpless child with limited choices, he had resorted to such attitudes as sensible and realistic attempts to cope with more than he could bear. Having been subjected to a detached father and a sick-room atmosphere created by his hypochondriac mother, he could hardly escape exaggerating his minor aches and pains, carrying them into adult life. Headaches, stomach rumbles, constipation, constant colds, back pains, eye irritations — all these pervaded his life. Ministering constantly to these feelings seemed much more comfortable than participating in normal activities. A healthy attitude was a threat.

As a teenager, he had developed devious coping strategies to save himself from a hostile home environment. He had spent countless hours with peers, drinking, taking drugs, and engaging in violent outbursts against his parents. He had miraculously managed to finish high school and college and find a job, which he kept sabotaging. His boss had accused him of irresponsibility and disorganization, and Harold had given the appearance of being contrite, promising a *change*. However, his familiar pattern continued until his services were terminated. He failed to realize that the once-upon-a-time *crazy attitudes* that, as a child, he had used for survival were preventing him from maturing. He failed to recognize how his adult environment differed drastically from his childhood home where he had felt so helpless. He failed to grasp the joy of freedom that comes from being able to take care of oneself and being able to behave in a responsible manner. He could not harmonize the unseen warfare within his dual personality.

At thirty-seven, he continued using old methods to solve his current problems. He continued his alcohol and drug usage. During his therapy, he gained sufficient confidence to experience a few glimpses into sanity, creativity, and a healthier lifestyle. He bought himself a racket and balls and began to play tennis, an experience he cherished. He took a class in sculpting, at which he showed much promise; and he met an interesting woman, whom he started dating. New horizons unfolded for Harold. However, within three months, the good feelings he was experiencing became threatening. Will these good feelings last? he wondered. Once more he felt inner discomfort. He became so possessive of his girlfriend that she left him. This was a devastating blow to Harold. It was too painful for him to confront his reality, to accept human limitations and behave responsibly in his interaction with other people. To quiet down the twin within, he indulged in grandiose fantasies. He became enamored with the idea of building a small airplane, which he would sell to a major company. He discussed the project with his acquaintances, who grinned at his fantasy and suggested he was in a dream world. Harold felt rejected, anxious, and unworthy. Connecting this feeling of anxiety with similar feelings he had experienced earlier in his life, he slid back into his old depressive state. Seduced by his feelings of failure and the belief that his life could not change, he deluded himself that an ongoing *happiness* was all he needed. On New Year's Eve, he had one too many of everything that he had been addicted to since the age of seventeen. He died.

We cannot help but recognize the great tragedy of Harold's case. Perhaps the greatest tragedy of the human mind, an impairment of morale, is summarized in a poem he left behind.

MOURNFUL WINTER

I will die at dawn of a mournful winter,
In a cold room where I have lived alone.

> I shall hear the rain fall as I wax away,
> And the noisy tumults of the highway.
>
> I will die at dawn of a mournful winter
> Among old furniture and empty bottles.
> By accident, someone will find me,
> A man unknown, they will bury me.
>
> Friends and peers, as they play cards,
> Some day they will ask, "What about Harold?
> Has anyone seen him? He hasn't been around."
> Another would reply, "Hal must have died!"
>
> They will all pause, drinks in hand.
> Sadly they will shake their heads,
> They may even say, "What is life?
> Yesterday alive! Today, dead."
>
> This death will end my dreams and pain.
> Parents, relatives a grief will share;
> They might offer memorial services,
> But I'm lucky I won't be there.

When we abdicate our own initiative we are like children who misbehave and anticipate punishment; an undefined guilt permeates the wind. It is not our high moral nature that produces guilt feelings in us; rather it is our fear of the opinions of others. People who are living fully on their own initiative and responsibility will not do anything for which they will later feel ashamed.

Erich Fromm makes a penetrating presentation as he deals with Mr. K's dullness in Kafka's play *The Trial*. He calls Mr. K's drifting, lack of autonomy, and growth "his unproductive living." As Fromm points out, such a person is bound to feel guilty and does so for good reason: he *is* guilty. He is always on the lookout for somebody else to solve his problems instead of turning to himself and his own resources. There is profound wisdom in this analysis. But I think it is incomplete. It does not consider the futility of self-accusations, their condemnatory character. In other words, it leaves out the point that Mr. K's attitude toward his guilt is, in its turn, unconstructive, because he deals with it in a spirit of self-hate.

Do you ever catch yourself undermining your own self-confidence? This is done by belittling, disparaging, doubting, discrediting, and ridiculing yourself. In subtle and gross ways, some people place insufficient value upon their time, their wishes, their work done or to be done, their opinions, their convictions. Such people have a compulsive need to compare themselves with everybody with whom they come in contact, and they do this to their own disadvantage. Their comparisons are not only unfair but often do not make any sense. The shining qualities of others tend to be in focus: they are more impressive, better informed, more attractive, more interesting, better dressed, more gifted. Comparing in this way is a form of self-shaming.

This focus on the betterness of others accentuates the person's nonacceptance of self. The thinking is processed thus: You are better than I am; I feel bad about me; I don't like me. Because this feeling of disliking me is uncomfortable, the tendency is to project it on others: I don't like me; therefore, others don't like me. As this feeling is externalized, it may lead to a subtle poisoning of human relationships.

What exactly do people despise in themselves? Sometimes everything, but most of the time they despise their human limitations. They focus not on qualities that they have, but on capabilities that they wish they had: physical strength, beauty of appearance, extraordinary intelligence, critical thinking, memory, organizing skills — any possible activity from simple private action to public performance. Lack of these is considered as *weakness* or *deprivation*. Such thinking confines a person to passivity and more self-contempt and frustration.

Somewhat different is Alison's situation, which illustrates another aspect of the twin within: the constructive forces. As a little girl, Alison was anxious and excitable. Her parents so pampered her that she had excessive confidence in her own judgment. That she had a keen mind none could deny. Alison used her mind with zest, thinking at high speed and deciding on impulse. At twenty-one, she was a tall blond with blue eyes and a healthy body. She dressed in the height of fashion, and Daddy paid the bills. The world owed her a living. Why not? There was someone around to feed her fantasies. For her there was no reality except a good time. As long as there was a man to take her out and shower her with goodies, everything seemed to go smoothly. Interpersonal relationships and courtesy toward her parents were not on her agenda because she was in love. After a year of passionate love-making, Alison's boyfriend gradually lost interest in her and decided to break off the relationship. He moved out of state, leaving no forwarding address. Alison found only the shreds of life were left. Her feelings of abandonment by her boyfriend joined those of not being loved by her parents, as she perceived it. She felt used, exploited, a lollipop having no more substance or sweetness. That is how she viewed herself, and that is a state of mind in which destructive forces thrive. Nothing meant anything to her anymore. Then she wished to punish the world and those in it, parents and friends. They could not make her happy.

Bottled up, the destructive twin within her chose a mechanism of revenge in suicide. Like a little child in a temper tantrum, Alison decided to destroy the healthy part of herself.

She was rushed to the hospital, where she was treated for an overdose of pills. The little note she left behind clued the shocked parents into the realization that she needed help. The overdose was not fatal. The content of the note surprised the parents: "Nobody cares; nobody loves me. Life is a lollipop; you suck it and it melts."

Alison's parents exhausted themselves in their efforts to persuade her that there was a better way of life than the one she was leading; that dropping out of school, sleeping around, and disappearing for weekends with boyfriends would not bring her happiness. They made no impression on Alison, and following a psychologist's instructions, they allowed her to make her own mistakes.

The therapist focused on the destructive forces that gave Alison the notion that suicide was an option.

"Life certainly seems illogical, incomprehensible, and often cruel," said the therapist.

"Blah!" Alison responded.

"Suicide ends the blahs," said the therapist.

After moments of silence, the therapist stood up, walked around her room, pulled down the shades, and turned off the lights. Alison did not know what to make of this; out of the corner of her eye, she watched her movements.

"This might seem like a strange or even silly exercise. But I have done it before. Trust me," she said. "Lie down on the floor."

Alison was puzzled, but she followed directions.

"Let your body go. Pretend you are dead. Your pills worked well and you never woke up. You are dead. You no longer have life in you. Your life has ended at twenty-one. Soon your funeral will take place. It is taking place right now. Your casket is open; the altar is abundant with flowers; the pews are filled to capacity."

After a long pause, the therapist continued softly. "Now I want you to approach those attending your funeral, and in an invisible way I want you to register the emotional and physical reactions that they experience. Are they looking at your body? How do they feel? Do they need consolation? Look at each of them carefully. Is there someone special in the congregation to whom you have something special to say? Could some of these be friends, perhaps a lover, your parents, a sister or a brother? Is there something you would like to tell them or explain to them? Is there someone you would like to put your arms around, expressing your love?"

There was a long pause.

"It's all over, Alison," said the therapist. "Death brought an end to your existence. Without your life you have no feelings, no power to move, no speech ability to express anything. You are dead. People have sent flowers — maybe some flowers you don't like. But does it matter? Someone is giving a eulogy. Is he telling the truth about you, or is he trying to comfort your parents? Does it matter? You have no feelings either way."

After a long pause, the therapist changed her tone and exclaimed affectionately, "Alison, come back to life!" Then she added gently, "Your funeral is over."

Alison seemed to come out of a daze. She sat up, moved her head from side to side, blinked her eyes, and smiled. She touched her heart. It was pounding steadily. She exhaled with a sense of relief. The therapist offered a hand as she got to her feet. She stretched her arms and sat on the chair. "It's a good feeling," she said.

"What's a good feeling?"

"That I'm not dead."

"I can't do anything for dead people." The therapist laughed. "But I can work with those who want to live."

"I want to live," said Alison.

During the sessions that followed, Alison began to recognize the constructive and destructive forces that are within everyone. She learned to be in control of the destructive ones by monitoring her thoughts and behavior. Simple questions to herself gave her some direction; for example, "Is this good for me?" or "How is this action going to benefit me and those around me?" She realized that all of us are capable of destruction, including the destruction of self. However, we have alternatives.

How many individuals find themselves in a state of mind in which they say, "I just can't go on"? What they really mean is that their current condition is unbearable, relationships are troublesome, and life is difficult. Instead of attempting suicide, could they take time off and go on a lengthy vacation? Could they leave the strain behind and move on to a healthier setting?

Alison chose to go to the Greek islands for a month. She made new friends and learned to dance the *hasapiko*, Zorba's dance. Furthermore, the blue sea, the rocky beach, and the simple life of the islanders gave her a message that she had a right to happiness. She accepted the message.

Harold's death and Alison's survival generate some questions:

- What is a person to do when the chips are down?

- When life becomes an impasse, are there any options?

- Is death an option?

- Is life worth pursuing?

When you look around you and everything appears hopeless, it is time to look into your self. As the ancient adage affirms: Go deeper into yourself and learn from within what to do. Very often the concept of *going into oneself* leads to emotionalism, because that is where the feelings abide. It is an essential step, but overcoming emotionalism follows that stage. With attentiveness to our inner and outer life and with objectivity, we can go beyond therapy. We become our own therapists.

Thoughts to Ponder

- How you feel about the world around you, that is, how you perceive it and react to it, is determined in large part by how you feel about who you are.

- If you see yourself as a maturing person — a person with adult aspirations and not mired down in childish concerns and infantile needs — then it will be easier to respect yourself.

- Having respect for yourself implies, at least, that you will not harm yourself.

- Growing up and growing older involve changing. Changing our attitude is an option.

- The very thing most of us want most of the time is change. We wish our situation were different.

- A real option is to face our problem and to focus on what we can do to change it, if it can and ought to be changed. Invariably there is a risk. Are you willing to take it?

- Can you harmonize your past history with the ephemeral reality of the present? Can you make friends with the twin within?

Chapter 5

Me Talking to Me

Dialogue is to life what blood is to the body.
When the flow of blood stops, the body dies.
When dialogue stops, life withers and resentment
and misery are born. Absence of dialogue means
death.

—*Ira Progoff*

Have you ever talked to yourself? Some people do. Others may think that talking to one's self is a sign of insanity.

I was taking a stroll early one Sunday morning in Media, Pennsylvania, a little town near Philadelphia. All the stores were closed, and I thought I was alone on the main street. As I was perusing the items displayed in a store window, I heard the voice of a little boy who was also standing in front of a window; he looked about six years old, and he was talking to himself. Around the corner came his friend. "Who are you talking to?" he shouted.

"Me talking to me."

"You must be nuts. How can you talk to yourself?"

"Come. Look. I'm talking to me."

I could not resist intruding; I stood beside them. The boy was looking in a mirror on display and was enjoying the conversation with himself. His friend pushed him aside, saying, "Let me talk to myself."

While the boys continued their chatter, I went on my way, thinking, What an idea! His naive answer, "Me talking to me," echoed in my ears. When I reached home, I looked at my reflection in the bedroom mirror and attempted a conversation, but I felt silly. There must be a better way, I thought. I do not need a mirror. I do not need to verbalize. I should have a silent dialogue with myself.

In the days that followed, I began this inner talk with myself and derived a great deal out of the few minutes that I invested. An example may make this clear. In my early thirties, I found myself confused and bewildered about the purpose of my life. I had consulted with spiritual leaders and psychologists, I had invested significant amounts of money in therapy, and I had read many books; yet no new direction was available to my conscious mind. During this period, I had a recurring dream in which I became blind. Then one day I drove to the beach and sat alone on the sand, watching the waves. The ocean breeze was soothing. I took several deep breaths and closed my eyes. The sound of the waves subsided, and I heard one word echoing within me: "Rectify! Rectify!"

"Rectify what?" I asked myself.

"The wrongs," answered my inner self.

"Rectify the wrongs?" I realized that I needed to understand this message. Uncertain about how to begin, which direction to take, I began to think about the implications of the meaning of the word "rectify." I entertained all kinds of possibilities, changes that I had to make, bad habits that I had to give up, initiatives that I should undertake. Eventually the idea came to me that my soul is God within me and that I should develop a dialogue with my soul. My dream carried a message. Blindness was a symbol. Not being able to see clearly the external world, I was being told to turn within myself and seek direction from my inner resources. As I began to cultivate this inner attitude, problems with work, family, and friends gradually began to fade. However, to make all this happen, it was first necessary for me to have sufficient determination to use my mind to think things through. I had to make an effort to rectify the wrongs wherever possible, listen to the inner voice, and maintain a dialogue with my spiritual self.

I let go of some old values that I held, such as expecting others to do things that I was capable of doing myself, expecting to be treated as someone special, seeking to do well and get recognition. These I replaced with new values. The world owes me nothing. If people do not approve of me or they judge me harshly, I tolerate the discomfort and continue to do the best I can. If I do not receive recognition for whatever I contribute to life, I get satisfaction in the process of doing what I choose to do.

One can be annoyed, troubled, perhaps even torn, by a sense of inner dissatisfaction, an inner division of two forces pulling in opposite directions.

- I know what is right to do, but I fail to do it.

- I do the opposite of what I intend.

- I know I can be a better person, but I don't know how to get there.

- I have a sense for the way things should go in order to be better, but I cannot translate it into a practical direction for my own life.

- I'm aware that the pulls of instinct and my social conditioning are often wrong and destructive, but I cannot quite see what to do instead.

It is as if we know that our present personalities, the sums of our lives as we have led them till now, are not what they could be. The task is one of discovering and developing a clearer contact with our inner source of wisdom. Frequently it is not easy to know where to start.

An extremely simple method within easy reach of most people can be used as a way of beginning. It is the technique of *dialogue with the inner self*.

Personally, I started with Epictetus, a Greek philosopher who said, "Humans are influenced and disturbed not by the events of their lives but by the way they view the events." I began to focus on how I viewed the world around me, how I perceived the events in my life, especially the ones in which I had been a participant.

No matter how bad things are, they do not cause depression. The moment we say things should be different, the thought evokes feelings of depression.

As I write this chapter, I recall a point made by Albert Ellis in one of his lectures: "If a runner loses a leg, his handicap does not cause depression. What he thinks and says about his handicap will cause depression. Feeling sorrow and sadness about the loss is normal. They cause the handicapped person to move on and do other things. The one who lost his leg can now learn to swim. He still has a choice."

The dialogue with yourself may start with your asking, "Why has it happened to me?"

INNER SELF: "It has happened."

YOU: "But it should not have happened."

INNER SELF: "Whatever occurred under those conditions, has occurred."

YOU: "It's terrible. I can't stand it."

INNER SELF: "Life could be worse."

No matter how badly we have done things, and we all do bad things, it is good to ask our inner selves, "How can we live and survive as happily as possible?"

In a world of inconveniences and discomfort we can truly find guidance by turning to our inner selves. Selfish? Not really. The technique of dialogue emerges out of the psychological studies of various philosophical and spiritual traditions. It is a practical application of the ancient and nearly universal belief that a human being has a spiritual aspect, a soul, and that this aspect can be contacted by the personality and asked for guidance. It has been said that the fundamental goal of psychology is the understanding of the relationship between the spiritual part of a human being and the personality. Those who hold this view call our attention to the root meaning of the word "psychology." In Greek, *psyche* means "soul," and so "psychology" implies the study of the soul. The science of psychology tries to understand our thought patterns, emotions and feelings, fantasies and daydreams, aspirations, dreams, conscious and unconscious motivations — in short, the full range of human behavior and experiences.

Psychological insight is a precious gift with which we can begin to understand ourselves. It does not come easily, but it can be facilitated by psychological knowledge, studying the inner self. This sort of study seeks healthy behavior, emotional wholeness, maturing growth, and ways we can rise above and beyond ourselves. Psychology challenges us to be more responsible because we have a dynamism, a spiritual aspect within our true selves, a real power. We cannot hide behind platitudes or camouflage what we must change in ourselves. To various degrees, we all have problems; we are all subjected to a common heritage and experience called "being alive." You may be troubled and overwhelmed by your problems, while I may be able to cope and manage mine. Other people handle their lives so well that we could mistakenly say they have no problems. The inner dialogue helps us to understand and to strengthen ourselves.

A school of psychological thinking different from the rest is Victor Frankl's logotherapy, which claims that our understanding of life and suffering depends on the meaning we find in them. "If there is a *why*, then we can find a *how*." The real issue of mental or emotional sickness in our times may not be neurosis or psychosis but meaninglessness. When we do not know the meaning of our lives, we wander aimlessly. We look in foreign fields to find the treasure, our health and happiness, although it is buried in our own backyard. Go deeper into yourself and discover. The only meaning there is to our life is the meaning we ascribe to it.

The technique of dialogue with the self is simple and direct. It consists of the assumption that within each of us is an endowment of wisdom, intuition, and sense of purpose, which can become a source of guidance in everyday life. The next step is simply to begin a dialogue with it, trusting that it is there and that it will answer.

Throughout history, when religious leaders were confronted with important issues, they withdrew from people and sought solitude. Once removed from worldly distractions, they consulted their inner world, their soul. When they returned, they were satisfied with the help of this inner guidance and felt they had found the best answer.

Spiritual people of past and present pull away from the crowds to pray or to communicate with their Heavenly Father, a sort of inner dialogue. The notion of having a dialogue with part of oneself that is attuned to the Divine is found in many religious practices; students of spirituality seek to distinguish lifestyles that are available, a choice between good and evil.

It is not by accident that Christianity anoints its followers in a ritual celebrating the *in-dwelling of the Holy Spirit*, validating the concept that the body is the temple of the spirit. The offered prayer seeks "whatever is good and beneficial to the soul."

Truly, once we exhaust all the ordinary and rational ways of wrestling with a problem, we need to turn to a higher source for an answer.

Practices such as this can be appreciated as attempts to contact another entity, an unseen resource full of power and wisdom. Or they can be thought of as attempts to reach those parts of our own psyche that are not available in our ordinary lives.

A dialogue with the inner self does not necessarily have to be a religious experience. A divine entity does not have to supervise it. It is enough to accept the entirely reasonable proposition that there are aspects in each of us that are higher and deeper than those of which we are normally aware. In short, it is enough that we believe there are in us positive human potentials for more wisdom, love, strength, compassion, and growth than we have yet discovered. If we believe these are accessible and that they can be explored, that is enough.

If the idea of a dialogue with yourself is new or strange to you, it may be worthwhile to begin simply by thinking through the reasonableness of the idea. One time or another, you may have had an experience that indicated to you that latent parts of yourself wiser than your daily self came to your rescue; for example, you encountered a difficult situation that you came through with a sense of success, or you solved a problem and felt good about the solution, or you faced a crisis with courage and determination. This kind of thinking—that you have your own inner strength — helps to quiet skepticism and the tendency we all have to repress the good and sublime within us, the higher self.

Most people who have accepted the notion of the higher self discover that over a period of time the inner self provides better answers, surer guidance, and more loving impulses. There are some people, perhaps because of temporary crises or a disturbed lifestyle, who have trouble giving themselves a chance. Either an exaggerated sense of guilt or a tarnished self-image holds them back from seeing the deeper regions of the self. Understandably, these may be people who hurt a great deal, and their pain causes them to be overconscious of their suffering. You may ask, "How much more can I hurt if I were to explore my inner self?" The answer may be, "not much more," because under the hurt lies healing. The following is a given:

we have inner healing power, at times incomprehensible to our human minds; the same power that heals the body heals the spirit.

A caution should be noted: in cultivating a dialogue with the inner self, we need to be careful to identify the voices that answer our questions. These silent voices must come from our authentic self, not from an ambitious parent or an angry coach or a demanding teacher. It is very important that we test any message that we receive with reality. To hear the authentic voice speak, we must listen with a genuine feeling of compassion for ourselves. To listen with the brain means to open a memory bank of painful messages. The brain, like a computer, draws upon what is stored in the memory, the dead past, known and unknown memories; not all of them are bad. Human potential lies in the realm of the unknown, the part of our unconscious that yearns to become known to us. Simply stated, we can ask, Is this advice really wise? Does it make sense in my current situation? It is equally important to challenge these silent messages to ensure they are not the result of wishful thinking.

In times of conflict, we need to be especially careful when the inner voices are many, all clamoring at the same time and creating confusion. In that case, we need to treat the answers we receive just as we would the advice of a good friend. We consider it, make sure we understand it, and try to decide whether it is useful or not. If the answer is really from the genuine self, our task is likely to be easy, because it will often have some especially heartfelt inspiration. This quality may be the very essence of common sense, or it may be diametrically opposed to all former values and beliefs. It may be a truly revolutionary break from the past. It may ask you to take a major risk. It may be a simplicity that is profoundly beautiful. The answer may be accompanied by a vision of the good that will come out of it, which becomes a source of joy. Then the course of action is likely to be clear.

If the answer clashes with our best values, giving us the notion that we might be hurting ourselves and others, then we can be sure that such an answer has a different source. It may be emerging from the false self. At best it must be scrutinized; beware, for it may have dangerous effects. Many cases of fanaticism, ego inflation, or delusions of grandeur are products of the false self. The danger may be there, but we might have to take that risk for the sake of change. This is the demon on the path to higher self. Assume that he may be there and then circumvent him.

Making contact with our own inner wisdom requires a vigilant participation of the mind. With the assurance that we have an inner core that is wise, good, and loving, we have a basis upon which to build a coherent program of self-development. We experience our intrinsic worthwhileness, and we hear its gradual and gentle call. We can then increasingly align our will, our intellect, and our emotional nature to fulfill the best that is in us. Intellect and will are instruments in service of the spiritual self.

Thoughts to Ponder

- Accepting the concept of an unexplored potential, intrinsic qualities that are good in ourselves, can mean the difference between success and failure, love and hate, happiness and bitterness.

- The discovery and development of the real self can transform victims of personality failure, recreate a faltering career, rescue a crumbling relationship.

- To develop a meaningful dialogue with another person, you must be able to maintain a dialogue with your inner self.

- To maintain a dialogue with yourself, you must have a self that you can trust and believe in, a self that you are not ashamed to be, a self that you can feel free to express.

- There is a spark within each of us, a soul that keeps us alive, a creative spirit that is forever working toward health, happiness, and all that makes for more life for the individual.

- Learn to trust your inner self, your creative and life-giving spirit, and let it do its work. Becoming too concerned or too anxious about whether it will work muffles the dialogue with your spirit.

- As much as possible, ignore completely and close your mind to all those pessimistic and negative thoughts that originate in your past.

- Make an effort to be less critical and a little more tolerant of yourself and other people in terms of faults, failings, and mistakes. See the glass as half full, not half empty.

Chapter 6

What Is Missing?

Self-observation brings humans to the realization
of necessity for self-change. In observing ourselves we notice that self-observation itself brings
about certain changes in our inner processes.

—*G. Gurdjieff*

Part of our human condition lies in a sense of personal inadequacy, a feeling that we are not quite right, an apprehension
that something is missing in our lives. In our efforts to interact
with people, we experience a sense of incompleteness.

No individual born into this world is so fortunate as to enjoy a sense of completeness at a given stage of his or her life.
The most effective parents do not succeed in convincing their
children that they are loved as real people in their own right.
Parents do not have to be grossly bad people to fail their children in this respect. The whole relationship between parents
and their children tends to intensify children's consciousness of
their own smallness, incompleteness, helplessness, lack of confidence, and fear of active venturing. Children become prey to
feelings of insecurity and inadequacy; they find difficulty in developing a sense of joyous confidence in spontaneous activity as
the years unfold. Later, facing the world becomes a frightening
experience. Of course, this feeling of incompleteness, which all
of us experience to different degrees, is not necessarily a disadvantage. It is natural and makes us eager to step out into the
world; it makes life possible for us.

The myth that completeness exists leads us to seek relationships — "people need people," as the song summarizes — an

attempt that often results in disappointment. No matter how hard or how long we try, we will never be complete. We cannot be complete as individuals; nor can we be complete by connecting with another person or institution or by marrying and having children, or even by becoming a star or a money magnate. Yet if we learn to accept our imperfections as part of the human condition and become aware of our own incompleteness, then we will be able to engage in healthy interaction with others. Our life will be a liberating and more pleasant experience.

Dave was a thirty-four-year-old physician unable to deal with people. He had a private practice and was attached to a hospital. He would have preferred to have been involved in research, for he viewed a laboratory as a haven in contrast to the hospital or his private practice office. He maintained the notion that if he were a disk jockey or radio announcer, he would be happier. But he did not seem willing to explore or pursue this fantasy. One rainy night, under the influence of marijuana and alcohol, he caused a serious automobile accident. Although the victim's car was demolished, the occupants miraculously escaped death. Dave received only minor scratches, and his Lincoln Continental was slightly dented. The medical insignia on his car and the pretense that he was on call helped to get him off the hook. The local medical association, which had other complaints about him on file, recommended that Dave seek professional help.

Although he was a difficult patient, Dave reluctantly began to recognize his destructiveness. He attributed his desire for drugs to a need for relaxation and to the pleasurable experience they induced. His capacity for mature pleasure was limited, and his inability to postpone gratification or control his impulses as well as his lack of compassion for others contributed to his inability to consider the consequences of his actions. Dave could recite the Hippocratic Oath by heart, but he had difficulty implementing Hippocrates' admonition, "Physician, at least do no harm." When I inquired about Dave's style of living and his way of relating to people, he avoided a direct response and did not admit that he had trouble in establishing interpersonal relationships. He treated people as objects serving his needs. Sex and drugs were opportunities that offered temporary relief from inner emptiness. Dave felt entitled to do what he did but admitted that others were entitled to disagree with his style. Although he attached minimal significance to others, even his colleagues, some general sense of respect from the world was important to him. He did work hard at the hospital, but when he was unable to gain appreciation from his patients, he felt increased loneliness and diminished self-esteem. Something seemed to be missing in his life.

I was struck by Dave's callous indifference to personal relations and was surprised by his being comfortable, apparently, while violating social and ethical norms. When he came for his fifth session, Dave was reading *Newsweek* in the waiting-room and came across the special report entitled: "Miami's Devastation." As he entered my office, he threw the magazine on the table, saying, "I don't understand why the media are making such a fuss over tragedies." After a moment's reflection, I observed the fear and anger in the doctor's eyes. What was missing in his life was causing loneliness and isolation.

"You must feel cut off from everyone," I said.

"I feel empty," responded the doctor, and after a deep sigh, he added, "I'm out of touch with my feelings. Inside I am numb. I seek out people who do not require me to be available to them emotionally. When someone says nice things about me, I don't believe them. I usually seek short-term sex partners. I just don't want to be involved."

The story of Effie can help us to understand such emotional and social deficits. Aged twenty-two, an unmarried college senior, Effie was an extremely pretty brunette who personified the young college coed. She sought counseling at the urging of her dormitory roommate who, along with Effie, felt that Effie might have latent homosexual tendencies. This concern proved unjustified, but other psychological characteristics clearly surfaced.

Effie rarely enjoyed herself on dates. She did not find herself disgusted or repelled with necking and petting, but she simply did not experience any pleasure in these activities — they had no effect on her. She avoided parties, preferring to stay in her room watching television or working at her studies. She was an excellent student who was majoring in geology, and she planned to have a career in forestry, petroleum research, or archaeology.

Effie was viewed by her classmates as distant and aloof. She rarely engaged in any social activity; she turned down an opportunity to join a sorority; she had no close friends — in fact, her only friends were her roommate and a girl back home. Despite her good looks, she was infrequently asked for dates, and when she did go out with a male companion, the relationship seldom lasted for more than two dates. Either the companion failed to ask her out again, or Effie refused the invitation. On campus, she was thought of as a "cold fish" and "a brain," someone who would rather talk about her courses and career plans than dance, drink, and have fun.

One relationship with a classmate lasted several months. He was a quiet, introverted young man who joined her in hiking expeditions; they discussed rocks and trees, a topic of mutual interest, and spoke disparagingly of the childish behavior of their classmates. After about ten hiking excursions, their relationship showed signs of faltering when they found they had nothing more to say to each other. Effie would have liked to continue the friendship, but she was not dismayed when it ended.

Further exploration showed that Effie rarely experienced joy or dismay or anger. She seemed content to let matters ride along, and she sat on the sidelines while others became perturbed, ecstatic, or hostile about unimportant trifles. This viewpoint, however, reflected less a well-reasoned philosophy of life than an inability to grasp what moved most people to be excited.

In describing her few relationships, past and present, Effie seemed to be vague, superficial, and naive, unable to organize her thoughts and tending to wander into irrelevancies such as the hairstyles, shoes, or clothes people preferred or the physical characteristics of their parents.

The illustrations of Dave and Effie, although not unique, seek to point out the dilemma of daily living when a person feels that something is missing. These two case histories focus on the reality of our human condition. We are not perfect or all-powerful or immortal. Dave was trying to find joy through erroneous efforts, by avoiding responsibility, exploiting other people, and abusing drugs. Effie, on the other hand, complacently searched books, archives, and archaeological mines; she had little interest in social relationships. She felt a thirst within that her current life could not quench.

Human beings remain essentially able to contact and to get along with others; we attempt to organize our private lives in accordance with requirements of larger-than-family organizations; we seek to find significance among other persons, pursue fulfillment of needs, both neurotic and normal, and personal gratification. The pursuit of pleasure often introduces a struggle for power and an effort to dominate others. We have not yet become more sociable and cooperative, as the optimistic theorists would have us believe; we have merely become more adept at exploiting the conventions of interpersonal relationships for our own benefit.

We can understand the rationale of self-adoration and alienation by taking a profound look within our own nation and across the world. Crime, violence, drug abuse, and exploitation create a climate of inner conflict and outer tension. We feel impotent, frustrated, despondent. "What's the use? Nothing ever changes. We're going down the drain." We hear statements like these and cringe with anguish. Then come the mass media to increase our insecurities with catastrophic headlines and shocking generalities. One glimpse at the news and many resort to primitive instincts of self-preservation: "Me first; to hell with the rest."

It is a disturbing feeling to realize that we cannot do much to influence mass media against capitalizing on the dramatization of the ills of our society: murder, rape, theft, and all sorts of political scandals.

Hollywood propagates hell on earth by producing lurid freak shows of ugliness and human depravity. In the last three years, acclaimed directors produced several movies depicting cannibalism. Two major releases involve incest. Are you not shocked rather than entertained or edified by going to a movie where you see sex scenes between a father and his teenage daughter, or a youthful hero and his panting, insatiable partner, his mother? Obscenities permeate our movies; foul language appears to be the most popular entertainment.

As mature adults, we can do only a little to bring about a change in a hostile and dangerous industry that haunts our lives daily, entering our homes every night to feed us violence, distorted sexuality, family deterioration, illegitimacy, infidelity, corruption — the pollution of our emotional and spiritual world.

Can we shield ourselves from such character-deforming trash? Can we write a letter to advertisers and let them know that we find them irresponsible in sponsoring television programs that are offensive to the general public?

It can be a devastating experience to see the world as it really is. We cannot overstress this point. Confronting the fact that we are finite, that we are not gods, that we have only limited control over life and its contingencies — each evokes frustration or anxiety. We think, we create, we soar up to speculate about atoms, space, and infinity, contemplating our own planet. We become aware of our splendid uniqueness, but we have a hard time accepting our grotesque fate — the moral and physical pollution of our planet.

Fantasy, wishful thinking, indulgence in artificial stimulation, or power plays tend to diffuse our anxiety about the fragile self. Once the implications of our natural incompleteness are accepted, however, the problem of our connecting with others is largely solved. We take a look in the mirror and we see an imperfect human being living an imperfect life among imperfect people in an imperfect world. Then we no longer look for perfection; nor do we expect it. There is more self-satisfaction in fulfilling our own humanity, limited though it is.

Start simply and steadily. We need to organize the world around us so that we may feel a part of it. As we learn to relate to other people, our presence in the world is confirmed. We feel less anxious. This external process of connecting with others, relating in a mutually rewarding manner, becomes easier when our internal world is in order, that is, when we have no guilt feelings, harbor no anger, wish no evil against anyone, have realistic expectations, and are eager to enter the world as mature adults.

To assume that individuals exist by themselves, that we are thrown into the world and abandoned to fate, is false. We have been born into a world of people, and we die in a world of people. We have never been on our own but have always been surrounded by potentially supportive, caring, and even loving human beings. If we accept that we are born into groups of people — families, friends, and peers — who may genuinely accept us and show us warm empathy and care, then we are not alone. We are reassured of belonging to a group, and not only can we develop the courage to recognize this group, but we can also actively and joyfully participate in it.

While interdependence is a fact of life — we depend on

some people for our existence, others depend on us for theirs — overdependence can make our life difficult. Healthy interaction implies that we do not manipulate people or become enmeshed with them. In establishing and respecting boundaries or limits as we interact with others, we gain a strong sense of relief.

The alluring fantasy that someone out there must be available to hold us together, to protect us, to provide for our needs, is misleading. It is an addictive expectation to be met only with disappointment. If we lean two dominos against each other, we have an unstable setup: if one of them moves, the other falls. If we perceive ourselves as half-persons, then we need someone to help us fill in the missing half; accordingly, our life tends to be turbulent and insecure. Temporarily someone may respond to our needs as an act of love or even of obligation; once we are grown, however, our well-being cannot be as fundamentally important to anyone else as it is to ourselves. Anyone who assumes a position of being responsible for another's well-being is subject to the corrupting temptations that come with that power. Even the most loving care, as demonstrated by parents in our early childhood, soon is subtly transformed into a controlling interaction that imposes what the donor believes the other person should have. The most altruistic giver can have ulterior motives.

When hopelessness and helplessness paralyze us, understandably we seek others to take care of our needs. In time of illness, we depend on science and medicine. But when our life is based exclusively on the needs of dependency, we may begin to think and believe that other people know better than we do what is best for us. Even with the best interests for each other at heart, the best-laid plans can result in hurt feelings.

A few weeks ago I watched a television production of John Steinbeck's classic story *Of Mice and Men*. Lennie and George, the two central characters, are powerful embodiments of an unhealthy type of interdependent relationship that has unforeseen costs. Lennie, huge, powerful, and moronic, depends utterly on his comrade and guide, George, for protection and warmth. George is driven into an extraordinary guardianship by the prompting of moral responsibility and a need for companionship. This relationship apparently cannot or will not lead to more traditional remedies for loneliness. What binds these two together is the picturing of an ideal future in which George and

Lennie will look after each other, save money, buy a house, own a cow and some pigs — a future in which Lennie can play with his rabbits and pet them. Lennie gratefully submits to George, assuming that George knows best what is missing from his life. The trusting dependency gives George power over Lennie, but George also feels burdened by having to look after Lennie. George complains that if he had no one to worry about, he could be happy and free. But the inference is clear: if he takes care of Lennie's needs, the time will come when they will live happily ever after.

It is worthwhile to consider a recurring scene: each time Lennie, in a childish and demanding manner, begs George to retell the story about the rabbits, the latter reluctantly gives in.

"Tell me — like you done before."

"Tell you what?"

"About the rabbits."

George snapped. "You ain't gonna put nothing over on me."

Lennie pleaded. "Come on, George. Tell me. Please. Like you done before."

"You get a kick outta that, don't you? Awright. I'll tell you, and then we'll eat our supper...."

George's voice becomes deeper as he retells the story that they both love so much. The missing parts are recovered. Lennie makes sure that no part of the story is left out. Gradually their fantasy ends in futility. Unwittingly, Lennie gets into trouble: he accidentally kills a woman. To protect Lennie from suffering from the consequences of his act, George decides to shoot him.

Like Lennie and George, many unhappy people destroy any prospects of what they might have. Unable to accept life as life is, they engage in daydreaming to pacify their inner turbulence. They create a life-enhancing fantasy in which to believe, and they desperately search for what is missing or for any experience that might make them complete. This search for the magical Garden of Eden, to find mates who love, friends who care, to connect with others who would fulfill their emptiness, is endless. Some people waste their lives in search of the good parents they once so much needed but never had. Others feel they would be satisfied if they met someone who knew the true meaning of life, someone who could explain the meaning of their misery. Could this be a psychotherapist? A charismatic guru? A holy person?

Such was the case of Sandy, a thirty-four-year-old mother of three beautiful children, who sought solace in a therapist's office. She was experiencing hurt, anger, emotional upset, and misery to a severe degree. Her husband, who was relentlessly seeking success, traveled much of the time, leaving her unattended. She considered herself as hopeless in a helpless situation; she was *trapped in a situation and mired in responsibilities.* The desire to change her husband's life consumed her. She felt empty within, and to diffuse this intolerable feeling she systematically focused on her mother and her two older sisters. One sister was divorced, and the other was involved in an affair with a married man. Since her father's death at the age of forty-two, her mother had been drinking heavily.

Recognizing that Sandy's overresponsible attitude sprang from her attempt to run away from her own emptiness, I said, "It must be terribly frustrating to attempt the impossible."

She calmed down and indicated a sense of relief. "A big piece is missing from the puzzle of my life," she said.

"Any idea what that might be?"

"No."

"Could it be that you feel powerless?"

"Powerless?"

"Yes, your control over your family's situation is limited."

"I should do something about my mess," she blurted out.

She had been engaged in a passionate affair with a twenty-year-old man who had caused her a great deal of pain, for he was unfaithful to her. Emptiness had taken over Sandy's life, leaving her in a state of confusion, guilt, and anger. The emotional connectedness with her family of origin was so slight as to be nonexistent.

"Go back to your family, not as a rescuer but as a human being, and stay there for a while," I said. "Later, try to connect with them in a creative way, accept their situation, listen to what they have to say, and share your situation with them in a nonthreatening and nondemanding way."

"I would rather commit suicide than go back to them," she replied.

I was not surprised. I could easily understand Sandy's reluctance to face an emptiness that was beyond her control. What brought significant relief was an art class. To be an artist was one of her early dreams that had remained unfulfilled because of marital obligations and responsibilities. Twice a week, Sandy attended an art class in a benevolent environment of classmates. The colorful classroom, the understanding instructor, and her participation helped to relieve her symptoms. Three months later, after the completion of a few paintings, Sandy began to see the connection between her problems and the emptiness that existed in her family, and she recognized that she had brought this feeling of emptiness into her nuclear family. What Sandy had expected of herself, an undefined anticipation, she had also expected from her mother and sisters. And there was a large gap between anticipation and reality. She had moved her anticipation into need and then into want. "I need more attention; I want more attention from my husband," she said. Her husband could not understand and responded with a "don't-nag-me" attitude. He was devoted to the demands of his corporation. Soon he was promoted, and his salary was substantially increased. To him, that meant success.

It is one thing to want something, another to expect it from an external source, and yet another to need it. If a want becomes a need and dictates the level of expectation — *soseme-mania*, the rescue-me passion — then the expectation becomes unrealistic and does not take reality into account. In Sandy's situation, her husband was a traveling salesman who was excited about his success. When Sandy came to terms with the reality that, at best, a married couple can only give so much to each other, she began to fulfill her needs with her own strengths. Her classes and a part-time job meant connecting with other caring individuals who became a supportive network. Although at times she still felt that something was missing, she better appreciated the human phenomenon. She accepted her own humanity, her own imperfections, and began to accept others as imperfect. This new perspective did wonders for her emotional attitude and fostered closeness with others.

The stories of Dave, Effie, and Sandy, so familiar in our times, bring to mind the characters in L. Frank Baum's tale, *The Wizard of Oz*. These troubled characters, whose problems touch familiar chords in our adult minds, are always looking for a helper or a guide. They are unhappy. Something is missing in their lives. They look for a helper to save them from their afflictions.

Dorothy, whisked away from her familiar surroundings by a cyclone, seeks help in the bewildering Land of Oz. While suffering confusion and distress, she meets with other unhappy creatures: the Scarecrow, the Tin Woodman, and the Cowardly Lion. If misery needs company, Dorothy has found it. They exchange complaints. Perched on a stick in a corn field and harassed by crows, the Scarecrow complains that he has no brains at all. He feels inadequate and foolish, but it is not his fault. He simply lacks what it takes to behave competently and wisely. "Don't expect too much of me; I am unable to think for myself and control my life."

Standing in the woods with ax uplifted in his hands, rusted and unable to move, is the Tin Woodman. As a man he has suffered so much and so often that he has to have all the parts in his body replaced. In the process, he loses his feelings. If only somebody would do something for him, he could possibly care for others instead of displaying artificial politeness. If someone does not oil him, he cannot function, but it is not his fault. The tin man has no heart. He can function but cannot feel. Neither relationship nor self-understanding is possible without a heart.

The Cowardly Lion roars and scares others, but at the slightest challenge he shows his cowardice. Although he has brains and heart and home, he lacks courage. So he makes it clear to his companions: Don't expect anything from me; I cannot act like a lion. Be careful not to frighten me.

Dorothy and her companions, the dissatisfied quartet, with some sense of genuine interest in each other's well-being, start their search for completeness. What is missing? they wonder. Each one has personal expectations. The Scarecrow needs brains instead of a heart — "For a fool would not know what to do with a heart if he had one." The Tin Woodman wants a heart — "For brains do not make one happy, and happiness is the best thing in the world." The Cowardly Lion wants courage — "For anything else is less important."

The Scarecrow cannot think. The Tin Woodman cannot love. The Lion lacks courage. In our pursuit of completion, heart and courage are needed ingredients. Without them, self-sufficiency and harmony of life are unattainable. As for Dorothy, she only wants to get back home to the familiar safety of her family, to her loving Aunt Em. It was satisfactory to return home. Home is a place where one is comfortable with one's self.

All four characters are demanding something from others, simple human qualities that they themselves already possess.

In their emptiness and unsatisfactory lives, they are searching to find someone somewhere to make them complete and happy. They eventually find the Wizard of Oz in Emerald City and expect him to fulfill their needs. After all, the Wizard is mighty and strong. They are helpless and inadequate.

Sensing their helplessness, the Wizard assigns a task. These poor helpless creatures have to kill the Wicked Witch of the West. Reluctantly they take on the task, and in the course of this adventure, they begin to feel genuine concern for one another. Now their mission has a meaning. When they come back to receive their reward, they still have not realized that they already possess what they expect from the Wizard. In the process of asserting themselves, they discover that the Wizard is a common man to whom they had attributed magic power. What they had expected from him, they each finally made possible for one another.

The Scarecrow learns that acquiring wisdom involves the risk of being wrong or even foolish. The Tin Woodman learns that being loving and tender requires a willingness to bear unhappiness. The Cowardly Lion discovers that courage involves the confidence to face danger, although at times fear is natural and permissible. Dorothy realizes that gaining freedom and power requires only a willingness to recognize their existence. The way to her inner harmony is possible if she accepts that all necessary ingredients exist within. It is her responsibility to search deeper into herself.

Once we learn to evaluate and temper our expectations of others, each of us has more time to devote to the self. As we pull back and take a realistic view of our expectations of others — what is it that I really want from this life? — we will have nothing to do but expect more of ourselves, perhaps a better performance or a healthier attitude toward others. As we place focus on self, we pleasantly discover that we are capable of contributing, and we discover what kind of contribution we can expect from others. We do what is possible, and we let go of what is impossible. We pursue what is good and worthwhile and avoid what is bad and possibly destructive.

Thoughts to Ponder

- **Accept** yourself as an imperfect human being. Allow space in your heart to accommodate the person that you are, with your strengths and limitations. Although you are similar to other people, you are different from everyone else.

- **Greet** each day with a feeling of gratitude. You are alive. Learn to care about your physical appearance. Clean and nourish your body. It is an irreplaceable instrument, so take good care of it. Your psyche is another part of you that keeps your body alive. Can you nurture your psyche with good reading, meditation, or prayer?

- **Acknowledge** that though you belong to a family, a mate or a spouse, or a group, basically you belong to yourself. Are you at peace with yourself, or are you in constant conflict? Can you get the twin within to be a friend instead of a rival?

- **Preserve** the purpose of your presence in life. Ask yourself if you are a consumer of goods or a contributor of goods. If life seems to have no purpose for you currently, can you give it a purpose even for this day?

- **Express** your feelings to someone that you find trustworthy — a friend, a relative, or an older person — in full awareness that no one can change your feelings or understand you totally. Can you, on your part, listen to someone who might want to talk to you?

As you focus on the acronym of the thoughts above, the all-encompassing word *AGAPE* is formed. *Agape* means "love." Our human reality indicates that we have limitations. As we start to make sense out of our personal lives, we need to love and cherish what we have, our *self* with its strengths and limitations.

Chapter 7

A Matter of Choice

> Human beings are changing all the time — hair,
> flesh, bones, blood, and the whole body. Which
> is true not only of the body, but also of the
> soul, whose habits, tempers, opinions, desires,
> pleasures, pains, fears, never remain the same in
> any one of us.
>
> —*Plato*

A human being is not a static entity. It is an organism in motion because it is in a constant state of growth; it is dynamic, a force seeking to express itself. Because that force exists in a welter of like forces, its natural mode is to strive to consolidate its uniqueness and affirm its self-determination. Put simply, your life is a process of organizing and mastering the elements in your world that are relevant to your existence.

This life force, emanating from the core of your self, expresses itself both instinctively and deliberately in self-assertiveness, in striving for freedom and mastery. The nature and quality of your life is the result of how you interact with the world around you. On one level, you want to organize, mold, influence, and master the objects and events of this world so your life can make sense. On another level, you are prone to yield to the world around you so you can become an organic and functioning part of something you perceive as greater than yourself. In other words, you are both an active organizer of your immediate environment and a passive participant in it. You belong to it, and it is bigger than you.

Obviously this recognition that we are participants in a

larger whole, in a bigger scheme of things, is essential to a maturing self. It enables us not only to move toward others but also to acknowledge and respect their *otherness,* accepting each person as a human being of worth, distinctive and unique, just as we are of worth, distinctive and unique. This attitude rules out possession, exploitation, and domination of the other person. Rather, it implies acceptance and understanding of the other's condition. What does this mean? Is it some sort of pop psychology that presumes to analyze everybody else's thing? Not at all. What it means is the *empathic imagination* to see the *real self* behind the face, the habits, the position, and the behavior of our fellow traveler through life.

Mr. Johnson lived to be very old. He attained great wealth, which his heirs will probably cherish and squander. However, he never attained any identification that took him beyond himself. He formed limited relationships, held the same job all his life, reared one child, joined a church, and occasionally contributed to charity. Yet he never actually identified with anyone. He used people, clung to people, dominated people. In the church setting, he professed love by irregular stingy offerings. He remained a closed-in person to the very end of his life. His pathetic perception of himself denied him real friends who could have made his life richer. At least they could have been present at his funeral. He lived alone; he died alone; he was a lonely millionaire.

Our ability to form and maintain sincere relationships depends on the strength and quality of our inner self. If you like yourself, others probably share your feelings. If you hate yourself, others dislike you. By liking yourself, I do not imply the narcissistic concept of infantile self-admiration in which the individual's love centers on himself or herself alone. You cannot really like yourself sufficiently unless you like others properly.

When you have learned to present yourself peacefully, with genuine interest in others, people will often feel tranquil in your presence. They will come closer to you, and your life will be enriched. People usually crave good company. They may mask this desire because they are afraid of rejection. Are you afraid of rejection? I am! I believe that most people are; however, the need to be close to others is universal. When you feel good within, you will feel the strength to be a loving person, and you will never feel alone.

People who are unhappy or emotionally disturbed either are unable to master their own life or are fear-ridden in relating to others. Either condition is detrimental to growth. Both can exist and thrive covertly. Like the most stubborn weeds in the garden, their roots go deep. They have their origins in early life; children instinctively indulge their freedom and their wish for mastery, or, unfamiliar with the strange rules by which adults play, they feel there is something wrong with them and that they are unlovable.

It is quite possible our whole problem can be traced back to this incipient and insidious feeling of worthlessness, that is, the fear that we are inadequate to master the situations that confront us and that we are undeserving of love and esteem. Of course there is an enormous variety of conditioning factors, any of which could lead to this loss of self-confidence and self-esteem. Let us explore a few:

1. If your parents tended to be anxious and insecure, they were probably overprotective, conveying to you a feeling that you lived in a world full of dangers with which you were inadequate to cope by yourself. By doing too much for you, they were convincing you that you could never do things for yourself.

2. If your parents were always overly eager to see that you did well, they were likely to be overly critical, giving you the uneasy feeling that "there must be something wrong with me; I can never do anything right."

3. And, of course, the other side of the coin: if your parents had a habit of distorting your achievements by exaggerating them, if they cast you in a superior role, always stressing their great expectations of you, they were actually sowing in you the seeds of self-derogation. Deep down, you knew your parents' picture of you was distorted. Nevertheless, it was against these inflated, often fantasy standards, that you unconsciously measured yourself and so fed the inward sense of worthlessness.

4. The endless "don'ts" that echoed in your ears as a child probably gave rise to the notion that the things you wanted most and enjoyed the most were the very things that were evil and thus taboo. Gradually you developed the secret anguish that you were essentially an evil person or, at best, below normal standards.

We are bombarded with negative messages throughout the growing-up process, though, of course, these are nicely veiled

in the cloak of protective love and rarely deliberate in their destructive aim. While these insidious little signals are never as
naked as the following list, it is what they really add up to.

- Don't be you...be us
- Don't be a child...
- Don't be grown up...
- Don't have your own existence...
- Don't have your own private feelings...
- Don't show your feelings...
- Don't think for yourself...
- Don't make it by yourself...
- Don't trust...
- Don't enjoy...
- Don't be too close...
- Don't...

Maybe nature equips the growing child with a sort of filter
for these endless Don'ts; we manage somehow to construct our
life patterns around them — a little like covering up scar tis-
sue with a Band-Aid — so that we can go on winning parental
approval and affection.

5. If, in the struggle to grow up, you were treated without
understanding and respect — whether this was the reality or
your fantasy — the chances are good that you reached the adult
world with deep fear that you were not equal to it. Having de-
posited little or nothing in the piggy bank of self-esteem, your
net worth was nil — by your own confused accounting.

If all this sounds familiar and you are saying to yourself,
"Right on!" are you not wondering why you were so ready
to accept the verdict of low net worth and never thought to
blame your parents for being so obviously lacking in understanding? The explanation is surprisingly simple. As a child,
your dominant instinct was to offset your natural weakness
with the assurance that your parents were both benevolent and
all-powerful. You clung to this belief beyond the stage when it

was useful, indeed necessary, to do so. It was more comfortable to stay with the emotional habit, even if it meant suppressing your individuality, unconsciously of course, in that daily exchange for security and affection and approval. However, by consistently overvaluing parental wisdom and power and thus confirming your overdependence on parental protection, you were seduced into this fatal bargain. Though never expressed so harshly or entered into so cynically, the terms of the bargain were almost Faustian in their implications: "You are weak and helpless against the world out there. We know all the pitfalls. Now if you are good, and if you love us as we love you, and if you do what we know is best for you and don't follow your impulses, we will take care of you and protect you."

It sounds absurd, overdrawn when stated like this; yet unfortunately a great many people carry this common curse right into adult life and go on feeling inadequate and unloved. The consequences are as unequivocal as the terms of the original bargain: to feel inadequate is to impair the will for self-determination; to feel unloved is to impair the capacity to love and accept others. It is a crippling blight.

If as a child you suffered too many emotional insults, you probably devised defensive strategies to reduce such affronts. You checked your initiative; you kept a tight lid on spontaneity. In short, you took on a protective coloration so your genuine self would not show. Nature does this all the time. Unlike a computer, there is a mechanism within for self-restoration, a natural intelligence that needs no therapeutic intervention. With sentient human creatures, this may result in a distortion of the original and true self and a subtle erosion of the will. If you have adopted a distorted concept of self, it is no wonder you feel like a straw in the wind, unable to act under your own power, always waiting for things to happen.

But we know all too well that *things don't just happen.* We make them happen. Outside conditions, changing circumstances, other people, all are factors. How we make these factors interact in our lives is ultimately a matter of the choices we make. We have choices, perhaps not always as wide a range as we might wish, but we do have choices. We may elect to go on feeling weak and unlovable, intimidated by a hostile world, and decide to withdraw from it and build a protective shell around us. This shell will eventually suffocate us. Or we may opt to revamp our attitude toward the world around us and explore whatever resources we have — probably some we have not even given ourselves a chance to discover — to construct a better life for ourselves.

Life is no rose garden. Life can, however, offer no end of interesting and rewarding experiences to those of us who keep ourselves open and accessible. The deadliest thing we can do to ourselves is to stay unavailable, self-enclosed, hermetically sealed against others, unable either to give or receive love. All love means in this context is that instead of keeping anxious watch over our own safety, we are willing to venture off that tiny island, go out of ourselves, and participate with others in that larger and more exciting life in which we have a rightful part. Life constricted to itself, isolated from the rest of life, is worthless. A priceless gem, radiant and alive in the sunlight, when shut in a box is colorless and dead. A human being is a social creature. Our life takes on meaning and delivers its rewards only when it is lived in this context, outside the confines of our individual self: when we are able to love others, that is, to participate with care and interest and delight in the lives of others; and when we are ready to be so loved in return.

We also have a choice about where to direct our anger. We may be angry with those who have wronged us, or we may express our anger at the world. There is a more appropriate target. Our anger will be creative and productive if we aim it dead on our own frustrations — if it is the kind of anger that says emphatically, "I will no longer stand for this! I would rather not be alive than be half alive, paralyzed by all these unreasonable fears, by all this psychic pain."

This kind of anger does not hurt; it cleanses. It is not debilitating; it is strengthening. The intense pressure it builds up inside can be put to very effective use in restoring our self-image, just as the powerful jet of steam that is used to blast the grime from an old building exposes the beauty and grace of the architecture. Our decisive act of restoration, however, is not merely cosmetic. As persons, we are in search of completeness. We are out in the world to reassert our integrity, reaffirm our priceless humanity, understand more clearly and appreciate afresh the unique qualities of our own nature. In the process of completing our selves, we will come to trust our thoughts, our feelings, our actions. There is no way we can continue to sustain the fiction that we are inadequate, unworthy, unloved, and unlovable. Like that once soot-encrusted, seemingly undistinguished building, our image will be resplendent in all the marvelous proportion and grace its designer originally intended.

Most of the time, our troubles are situational, but worrying is always a state of mind. Accepting painful experiences openly and honestly eliminates needless suffering. Whatever your current issues are, would you be willing to work on yourself, to take on a personal interest in improving your situation? It is truly your destiny and mine to grow among imperfect humans. Our families are imperfect, and most of them are dysfunctional. As a result, we are imperfect people. Either we are heirs of our progenitors' errors and have a genetic proclivity to be unhappy, or we share the ills and injustices of our current times. How we deal with life is our choice and challenge. Is alcohol the answer? Are drugs the answer? Can we afford to run from therapy to therapy to pacify our frustrations and disappointments? Perhaps we ought to explore what approach others use. Would their approach be useful to us? What about your approach?

Thoughts to Ponder

- *Badness:* When we focus on an ugly element of the self and believe that we are bad, this sort of feeling becomes a two-edged knife, cutting us and cutting others. If we do not like ourselves, how can we like anyone else? The discomfort that this feeling of badness causes within propels us to seek badness in others, and either we become judgmental or we feel guilt for our thoughts about them.

- *Dependency:* "Please, someone, look after me" is the cry of dependent persons. "If I could only find someone who knows well the true meaning of life, someone who would direct me and take care of me, a magic helper I could depend upon, I'd be happy." This sort of fantasy is called *soseme-mania,* passion to be saved by another.

- *Dissatisfaction:* As the retaliatory fire burns, we become incapacitated, unable to find satisfaction in other areas of our life. We cannot give or receive love, for we have become addicted to angry feelings. Our punitive attitude alienates us, and potential friends fear us and avoid our company.

- *Fragility:* When we have the feeling that no one loves us or when we are afraid of losing someone's love, we resort to manipulation. That is, we comply and conform with the wishes and expectations of others although we do not agree with them, lest we be rejected. It is an oversensitive and restless state of being.

- *Projection:* We often project negative feelings onto others. Unable to tolerate the feeling of negativity, we project it onto another individual, in the way a picture is projected onto a white screen. Seeing what you do not like about yourself, you punish yourself by inflicting your dislikes upon another, at times hurting unintentionally.

- *Retaliation:* There is a fierce desire in most of us to strike back: "Now that I feel stronger, I'll get you." Having been severely punished as children, we dream of sweet revenge, at least to get even. If our parents are not around in our adult life, revenge may be directed toward others.

- *Vulnerability:* Residual weakness and helplessness prevent people from ever feeling grown up. They remain embedded in nostalgic longing. It is not a matter of retaining childlike spontaneity but rather of holding on to the childish insistence that someone must take care of one who is so helpless. If there were such a caretaker, how long could you endure his or her dominion?

Chapter 8

Loneliness or Aloneness

> We make ourselves lonely. We do so by the way
> we remember our past, by the way we tell stories
> of what has happened to us, by the way we give
> up any hope of changing. If we make ourselves
> lonely, we can also make ourselves loving.
>
> —*Douglas Morrison and Christopher Witt*

Do you ever feel *lonely*? What is that feeling like for you? Nobody is around. There is nothing of interest to do. Your phone does not ring. No one calls. Two days go by. You have no place to go. You experience mild symptoms of edginess, tenseness, or nervousness.

Do you ever feel *alone*? How does it feel? In a time of joy or sorrow, somehow your friends disappear. You call them, and there is no answer. An uneventful week goes by — not even a postcard in your mailbox. However, you are not anxious.

Is there a difference between feeling lonely and feeling alone? Truly, there is, although many people mistakenly believe that the two words refer to the same condition. If we understand the differences between these two conditions we can confront them effectively.

Loneliness is a sign of our greatest vulnerability. Loneliness exercises a strong influence in discouraging our adult minds from growing up. As children fear the dark, many adults fear to grow up and assume responsibility for their life. They seem to cringe back from a wider consciousness and fail to initiate any sort of activity, preferring isolation from life.

Loneliness is often evoked through experiences of rejection

and feelings of guilt for not being who we are and for not ac-
tualizing our potentialities. We feel lonely when we suffer a
significant loss, when we are in the presence of tragedy or illness or death. We feel lonely when we are confronted with
a new truth that suddenly shatters our perceptions or ideas.
Regardless of how masterfully we try to discount the pain of
loneliness, it still hurts, and we recoil into our isolation.

In a society that values strength and independence, we like
to appear brave and strong. Initially we block out the pain of
loneliness by denying it, by dulling it with alcohol or drugs,
by hiding from it as we immerse ourselves in work and never-
ending activities. We do not want to admit that we are lonely,
for it makes us feel as though we are failures, as though there is
something wrong with us.

If we are not mentally retarded, physically handicapped, or
incurably ill, there is nothing wrong with us. We are not failures; we are human. Although loneliness hurts, we choose to be
lonely because we are afraid of something that hurts even more:
rejection. Instinctively, we protect ourselves from the awful possibility of being rejected, and we do so in ways that leave us
lonely. We react to people and events without much thought or
self-awareness.

Larry, a tenth grader, writes: "Loneliness is a depressing state
of mind that none desires but we all endure. When I'm lonely,
it's not because of being shut away from human beings physically but rather because of feeling rejected by those I respect and
love. Sometimes my own friends seem unfair; there is no one to
turn to, and I feel lost. I experience loneliness almost every day.
When someone makes a thoughtless criticism that attacks one
of my weaknesses, it takes the wind out of my sails. I wonder if
what the person says is really true. I feel very small, and that's
a kind of loneliness."

Lisa, a ninth grader, experiences loneliness in a different way.
She writes: "Loneliness gives me a cold feeling, like the loneliness the earth feels in the winter when the birds and flowers
have left her, and I feel as though I don't have a friend in the
world. The whole house is lifeless and that makes me feel depressed. Depression is truly a part of this feeling of loneliness.
It has no joy or excitement in it, as houses blessed with a happy
and loving family have. There never seems to be anything to
do. It all seems to be done; it is as if I were trapped in a strange

world of loneliness, a world in which I am caught up in a great vacuum of emptiness."

Loneliness, as experienced by both Larry and Lisa, is the emptiness they feel in their dependent attitude, when they have no one on whom to lean for comfort, entertainment, or support.

Lonely people have not learned how to occupy themselves in an interesting, productive manner. They seek someone who will accept, amuse, divert, distract, and reassure them so that they will not become aware of their inability to face the world alone. In short, they seek baby-sitters. They have not trained themselves to take the initiative, to invent activities of their own, to build, to make, to discover, to explore, and to improvise in the world around them. They seek someone to take them by the hand and lead them into greener pastures of enjoyment. When they can find no one to make them the center of their support and attention, they come into contact with a deep and abiding loneliness.

Such individuals usually find it difficult to establish any enduring relationships. Because they are so nonproductive and shallow in their lives, others find them boring companions and avoid them when possible. They demand so much and give back so little. As a result, they are thrown back upon themselves, which reinforces their loneliness. "Nobody cares," they say, as they wallow in self-pity, attributing their condition to others. Because they lack a basic sense of self-worth, their situation does not improve.

Teenage years tend to be the loneliest time. Young people begin to question the important connections in their life: their family, friends, values, and activities. They suddenly realize that their fantasies, daydreams, and ambitions are all games they have been playing and that have been played on them. They become aware that everything they considered real is not real anymore. They no longer know the people they live with or the places that have been important in their world; they do not know who they are anymore. The crisis of awakening to their loneliness and doubt is frightening, and so they withdraw deeper and deeper into themselves, trying to figure out what they can trust as real, whom they can rely on, and who they are.

This was Larry's experience when he dropped out of school. He retreated into a private world of questioning and doubting, listening to music, and searching for answers in his own dark room. He was angry at his teachers for their lack of understanding, and he avoided confrontation with his parents. Isolated, withdrawn, lonely, his confusion increased, and the fear of total dissipation of self overwhelmed him. He began to think that nothing mattered: "The world is cruel and full of cruel injustices. I might as well pull the plug," he said. Now he understood why some people end their lives. For several days he remained in his room with little to eat, in a state of inertia.

Then one day Lisa showed up on his doorstep. She wanted him to draw a cover for a school project. Larry excelled in art. She sat nearby, watched the artist at work, and waited. As Larry began to pencil a sketch, he became aware of Lisa's interest in his drawing. He felt her presence. His eyes filled with tears. Someone was genuinely interested in him, in his art, and this gave him a feeling of warmth. Their communication was silent, but a feeling of trust began to grow between them. When he finished the cover, she gave him a peck on the cheek, and he felt connected with another human being. He knew he could trust Lisa. He decided to walk her back to her house; few words were exchanged on the way. This was Larry's first time out of his room in a week. He felt a new energy and a desire to live again.

Gradually, Larry made some real contacts with other people who responded favorably to him. He discovered that in reaching out to make contacts the risk of disappointment was present, but he learned to take it. In the process, he came out of his lonely state. He realized that there was no reason for him to be alone; he discovered what really matters is giving new meanings and directions to one's life.

Any time we talk about ourselves, think about what has happened in our life, or relate the events to another person, we selectively recount stories of events that have influenced our thinking today. We all have stories which are particularly important to us. We are impressed by them, or we would like to impress others with them. When I report to you: "This is what I am doing today," or "This is what I did yesterday," I am actually saying, "This is who I am and why I do what I do." The events themselves — as critical as they may be — have less power over us than we think. Yesterday's fortunate or unfortunate event has no power over you. It is the way you recall or dramatize the event that gives you a certain kind of feeling.

Our stories of the past fashion our vision in the present; they determine how we see ourselves and others and what we expect of life and the world. Memory tends to be selective. It picks on painful events and negative experiences, either because they have left a lasting scar or because they are painfully dramatic. No life was all bad, though selective memory may portray it so. A client of mine had the habit of repeating the story of her childhood, relating events of mistreatment by her stepmother. At an opportune moment during one of her recitals, I said, "She must at least have changed your diapers; otherwise you would not have survived." Stories have power that shape our thinking, and we need to be careful how we tell them, or else they will lock us into the current state of mind that can remain as unchangeable as the past. When we allow our past, especially our unhappy history, to determine how we see ourselves in the present, we limit what we can do and how we can relate here and now.

Stomaotitis, which means "words come out of the mouth, go directly into the ears, and are believed to be the truth," is the word that I use for people who suffer from such a notion. When I say: *I am what I am because of the way I was raised,* or *because of my ethnic background,* or *because of things that happened to me,* I reassure myself that I have no other choice: "I am what happened to me in the past. It's not my fault, and I can't do anything about it."

Think for a moment about *stomaotitis* and challenge the notion, your belief system. Maybe there is *something* that you can do differently to *change* your current condition of loneliness. Every week, I see a man swimming at the local YMCA. One of his legs is amputated above the knee. He used to be a runner. He accepted his accident as a tragedy, but not as a total catastrophe, and he chose a healthy outlook.

It may sound depressing to think that we are the ones responsible for our own loneliness. How could we cause ourselves so much pain? What good is there for us if we remain in such a condition? And yet, admitting our part in making ourselves lonely gives us a lot of strength to choose a new direction. If we make ourselves lonely, we can also make ourselves reach out.

Incomparably different from loneliness, *aloneness* is a return to one's own self. When the world around you has grown cold and meaningless, when life has become too many demands and expectations, aloneness is a desired state to enter. You are no longer lonely; you are alone, a time of dialogue with yourself, a personal time for self-inventory and evaluation.

Alone, you are in this world, but you are not of this world. Each moment is studied and understood under a different light. When people are alone, they have a chance to examine the real nature of their existence. They become aware of the emptiness of their lives and discover that what really matters is taking a new direction.

I witnessed a mother's ultimate affliction. One year after her husband's death, she lost her only son. John was eight years old and needed open-heart surgery. The little boy died in the recovery room. I remember his mother the day of the funeral when relatives and friends came to offer their respects. She stood in front of the coffin and stared at the child, oblivious to anyone's presence. She did not hear their grief-stricken voices, she did not see their mournful faces, she did not hear the chanting of the priests and the nervous coughing of the congregation. She was alone with herself — the beating of her heart, the initial images of her son's birth, life in the crib, the rich moments when he began to make sounds and form words. Temporarily, she had reached the very bottom of her pain, but at the same time, there was a feeling of being near her son — the life and love they had both experienced in the last eight years. With a sigh of joy and sadness, she repeated to herself: "Oh, Johnny, how much I love you!" Her words were drenched in tears.

In solitude, we break through the experience of death, transcend the static pattern of life, have an opportunity to see life as it really is, and become aware of a desire for new meaning and vitality.

Alone and away from daily routine and disenchantment, we discover the path to ourselves, to our destiny. This new direction affords us a vision, hope, and excitement.

Aloneness is the independent *inner life* when we have finally shut our ears to the competing voices of external authorities, those who wish to influence us. Our own desire to influence them, in turn, is no longer of value to us. When we let go of our own control system, our desire to impress and compete, dominate and exploit, our need for personal recognition and the other remnants of our childhood, then the *inner voice* will be quite clear. A whole new world will open up inside us. Everything around us will come to life with a nature of its own. Our vision will be clear and we will accept things as they are, without a desire to distort, improve, modify, or change the outside world at all.

Aloneness, then, is a fullness of spirit, a state of grace, and knows no feeling of want, poverty, or discomfort. Loneliness is the empty world of seeking outside fires to warm us. It is children who have lost their parents in a crowd and are terrified by their lack of knowing what to do. On the other hand, aloneness is complete. Children feel secure in their parental arms.

A first step to enter this state of aloneness is to cut out some of the distractions, to simplify our life. Understandably, total retirement is not possible. We cannot shed our responsibilities. We cannot permanently inhabit a private room. We cannot be a monk or a nun in the midst of a family setting. We would not want to be. The solution may be attained neither in total renunciation of the world nor in total immersion in it. Perhaps there is a balance somewhere or an alternating rhythm between these two extremes, between aloneness and loneliness. When we take time out to be alone, we will learn something to carry back into our worldly life.

A second step may be getting rid of some gadgets. Let us look around our room or our house or our garage. Examine the things that we have accumulated over the years. Ask yourself: "Do these objects facilitate or hinder my life?" Most of these things are useless, but we hold on to them in the hope that some day they might be of value to us. Could these be the lifeless, neurotic attachments that clutter up our lives?

Cleaning out the external clutter gives us a clue to how to start the inner process of gaining clarity of mind. Simplification of outward life is not enough. It is merely external, but it gives us a technique, a road to grace.

As we shed some of our belongings, we can take a parallel step to rid ourselves of dishonesty, hypocrisy, and the desire to impress others. What a relief this can be, when we unclutter our minds from emotional hang-ups, anger, jealousy, hostile feelings, and old grudges. We may have noticed that the most emotionally exhausting thing in life is not being sincere.

Many theorists claim that loneliness lies at the heart of mental illness. We know that it causes isolation and pain. However, making a transition from loneliness to aloneness, we can harvest many benefits. Most of us are so frightened of being alone that we never let it happen. If family, friends, and movies should fail, there is still the radio or television to fill the void. Instead of planning time out to be alone, where our soul may blossom and thought may emerge, we choke our space with continuous music, chatter, and companionship, to which we pay little heed. They are simply there to fill the vacuum. When the noise stops, there is no inner music to take its place. We must relearn to be alone. Once we accomplish that, we realize there is a quality to being alone that is incredibly precious. Energy rushes into our soul; we feel richer, lucid, fuller than before. There is a quality to fullness that is best expressed by the psalmist: "My cup runneth over."

Thoughts to Ponder

- In a state of loneliness, you may indulge in fantasies that someone out there could sweep you off your feet and save you from the mess that exists within you.

- When you feel bad about yourself — inept, inadequate, incapable — do you really believe that another person can meet all your needs and diffuse your loneliness?

- Could your state of loneliness be your choice? You may be choosing to be lonely, although it hurts, because you are afraid of rejection.

- If you are afraid of rejection, as most people are, you may have a tendency to reject others, thinking it is better to walk away from them before they reject you. So you choose loneliness.

- Sometimes when you feel that something is missing in your life, something is lost, it is time to take a journey into yourself to explore the core of your being. This journey is not a lonely one, although you have to take it alone.

- Your life's story may not be a pleasant one; it may not be sweet or harmonious, as some invented stories are; yet it is your story, and that is important. How you decide to rewrite it is your business. You have a choice.

- Choose to be alone sometime during the year, some part of each week and each day. It is not an impossible task. If I could convince you that a day off or an hour alone was a reasonable ambition, you would find a way of attaining it.

- I cannot emphasize enough that you need this time out in order to find, again, the true essence of yourself, the core of your being, which is your greatest strength. Ask yourself: *What is it that keeps me alive?*

Chapter 9

Making a Contact

> We choose to be lonely even though it hurts
> because we're afraid of something that hurts even
> more: rejection.

> —*Douglas Morrison and Christopher Witt*

Every day we emerge from our inner sanctum — a physical, psychological, and spiritual space — to make contact with someone. If we emerge from a harmonized self, we look for a solid person with whom to start a relationship. If we emerge from a weak, fragmented self, we look for another fragmented person with whom to identify. Whatever the case, a human being is like a complex musical organ that produces harmony or cacophony. Human interaction depends largely upon the ability of two humans to harmonize. If we care to develop emotionally and feel at peace with our inner self, accepting human complexities — strengths and limitations — relationships with others will be rewarding. This inner harmonization is basic to all other relationships, for our respect for others is dependent upon our respect for ourselves. As we approach a person, we must not ignore our own humanness, for if we do so, we will harm ourselves and end a potentially good relationship by a bad start.

Our first few minutes with a new contact are very significant in establishing a relationship. Within our lifetime and space we exercise the prerogatives of our own personality, moving in a common area where the rights of others need to be considered and where adaptability is required.

An aggressive person may overpower the other by controlling or monopolizing the conversation. A narcissistic type of talk — relating our own accomplishments, aspirations, successes, and grandiose plans without allowing the other to insert a word — may bore or arouse jealousy or anger in the listener. The message conveyed is: This is who I am; this is what I want; who you are and what you want are of lesser importance to me — or of no importance at all.

If, in spite of being such a person, we are admired or envied and we prevail in the relationship for marked periods, behind our outward behavior will lurk feelings of emptiness and self-alienation. These dark feelings will come to the fore as soon as our image of grandiosity fails, and this will occur as soon as we are not on top to dominate the relationship. Then we will feel alone and inadequate.

Recounting his earliest recollections, Robert, a thirty-six-year-old accountant, said that he thought little of himself as a child. He claimed that he was a manipulative child who had no respect for others and was successful in coercing them into doing whatever he wanted.

Robert could not remember the presence in his life of persons who could give him love and acceptance. His mother was emotionally insecure, and her feelings of love and acceptance were conditional. He had to behave *her* way if he was to receive her affection and support. Since there was no husband at home, her insecurity took on the semblance of authority. Ignoring his needs for admiration, love, and approval, she made the rules and expected little Robert to obey them.

Had Robert been able as a child to express his true feelings toward his mother, to experience his rage and anger, he would have remained alive emotionally, but that behavior would have cost him the loss of his mother's love. He repressed his feelings and, with them, a part of himself, in order to preserve his object-relation.

In an adult, the repressed feelings are mirrored in relationships. For Robert, at the center of his fantasy is always this wish: "I wish someone would love me as my mother should have and did not." Thus, he searches for that *lost love* among people who could conceivably be searching for that same love.

Robert's situation, rooted in lack of parental care and support, resulted in frustration. Others refused to give him that initial motherly love. He was quickly dropped when he made

unreasonable demands. Chronically dissatisfied, he came to believe that the human environment was basically inimical and
that basic relationships could not satisfy emotional needs. Since
he lived in a world of people, out of necessity he learned to
manipulate others in the hope that they would respond to his
needs, but he could not engage in a normal relationship for the
long term.

Could Robert ever learn that people can only be manipulated
for a while? Once they discover the manipulating games, they
resent the manipulator, or they get angry with him or her and
resist the blandishments.

An aggressive approach to relationships, regardless of where
it originates, makes manipulation inevitable. If we can, we must
exploit, and the exploitation continues until the other person
moves away.

As we mature, we develop healthy defense mechanisms that
enable us to face people and situations with a sense of boldness,
without a chip on our shoulder. When we are confident in ourselves, we do not have to start a war to defend our position. We
are entitled to a lifestyle of our choice, and, while we maintain
our convictions, we do not have to impose them on others.

An assertive person maintains self-respect by pursuing the
satisfaction of his or her needs and safeguarding boundaries
without abusing or dominating or invading the privacy of the
other. Such behavior means that we possess a considerable degree of confidence and acceptance as to who we are — human
beings with abundant qualities, strengths, and weaknesses. Relating to others requires a sense of creativity: each person
contributes colors and elements to the tapestry of the contact.
Allowing the other person to unfold in his or her unique way,
without judgment on our part, and responding with undivided
attention show that we care for that person. If we approach the
other with a judgmental attitude, even when we do not say a
word to this effect, we can be sure that our contact is defective.
The other person's emotional antennae will pick up our negativity, and he or she will respond in a limited way. Of course,
some people are able to radiate a genuine interest in our approach, and such response makes us feel better about ourselves
within the initial contact. Others may not be as responsive. If
we maintain the contact without making demands, we may discover a wealth of positive qualities in the other person. When

we plant flowers, we do not expect them to survive unattended. If they are placed in proper soil and watered and fertilized, they will blossom and grow abundantly. Nurturing a relationship by considering the importance of the other will unquestionably yield a more productive interaction than neglecting the person.

Everyday living, every experience, every relationship provides us with an option of how to relate to another person. The choices are two: healthy or neurotic interaction. Either extreme can be destructive. Rewarding relationships are based on a healthy self, caring for the well-being of the other as well as for the self. Solid relationships with others result from our constantly confronting ourselves and our own humanity and exercising our good qualities responsibly. A responsible relationship depends upon a keen awareness of our emotional self and of the emotional self of the other. Like strings of a guitar, we must be carefully tuned to each other's awareness to produce harmony.

Individuals approach others in three distinct ways: identification, object relationships, and transference.

Identification: Identification refers to an intrapsychic mechanism in which individuals associate themselves with another person, usually as a means of enhancing their feelings of self-worth. Let me illustrate with a personal experience. After hours of waiting in line, my wife and I were seated at a table in a New York restaurant. I noticed how sweaty and fatigued our waiter appeared. Experiencing a rush of sympathy because I had once worked in a similar type of restaurant in Philadelphia, I said, "Working in a restaurant like this must be very difficult during holidays." The waiter replied, "Yeah, some people are so damn demanding, they think they own you."

Without giving consideration to this waiter's individual circumstances, I had expected his feelings to be similar to my own so that I could meet him on common ground. Such sharing of fellow-feeling is known as *identification*. Often an approach of this kind serves as a beginning for people to get together.

An interesting parallel phenomenon that characterizes people's behavior in relating by identification is the *neurotic attachment*. Weak persons may identify with someone strong to bolster their own sense of importance. Or strong persons may identify with the weak to gain mastery or confirm their superiority. The genuine identification that mature persons are able to make after they have become reasonably well acquainted with the other checks this process and restores the proper balance.

Object Relationships: This is an unconscious process, relating with others according to the images of our past. Infants internalize images of the good mother and the bad mother according to how adequately their needs are satisfied by parents or adult figures who act as parents. In adult life, when they meet another person, the images of earlier experiences may influence the relationship. We unconsciously analyze and evaluate people as objects. That other person must be kept individual and separate from our images. We must think: "This is John, my friend. This is not John, my cousin who loved me [or hated me] when I was young."

If we are mature people, we find satisfaction, as the relationship develops and grows, in our increasing capacity to refrain from judgments and in pursuing the attitude of acceptance. Along with such an attitude, another characteristic is found in object relationships, and that is the willingness, even desire, to understand the other person. Mature relations are two-way relations between emotional equals and are characterized by mutuality, spontaneity, cooperation, appreciation, and the preservation of individuality in interaction.

An emotionally healthy person allows maximum interaction, supported by feelings of self-esteem, pleasure in success, empathy in failure, creativity, humor, and prudence. Tuned in to inner harmony, we can be open without fear of being crushed, expressing opinions without crushing others. It is at this point that men and women can love and respect themselves enough to allow a moment of being wholly and deeply touched by another human being. Each goes on being and becoming because of what the other is being and becoming, in personal interaction and mutual unfolding. It may be compared, perhaps, with the desire for mutual understanding that prompts two people who are only slightly familiar with each other's language to attempt to enlarge their capacities for communication by various indicators and signs, such as giving each other quality time or discussing personal issues that are serious. It implies a warm and active effort to know the other person by participating in the other's world.

Another characteristic implicit in object relationships is *stead-*

fastness, that is, the providing of an anchor for the relationship. When a person is willing without fickleness to encourage and foster the relationship with the other person, not disrupting it except for good reason — a reason mutually understood or at least communicated — that anchor is established.

Transference: This word is popular in our times of psychological analyzing. In therapy, there comes a time when clients tend to generalize attitudes and feelings learned in relation to their parents and cast them upon the therapist. Unconsciously, clients relate with the therapist as they would relate with a parental figure. This tendency lingers on into adult life; two people develop a relationship and one or both of them see in the other a significant person of past life. Visualize yourself going to the bank once a week. You seem to gravitate toward the same teller. You realize this teller bears a remarkable resemblance, not only in appearance but also in mannerisms, to your sister. During your banking transactions, you perceive in yourself a strange, persistent notion that this woman, whom in reality you know only slightly, should respond to you as if she were your sister. Finding yourself unable to avoid the thought that she might greet you affectionately, as did your loving sister while you were still under the same roof, you continue to carry an image, a fantasy that is irrational and that could result in disappointment.

It is obvious that if we indulge in reveries that permit relationships to begin on such a basis, the chances of maintaining them are slim. The bank teller, for instance, is not your sister; she has not shared family history and developmental experiences with you. Consequently, she is not able to respond to your needs on the basis of your fantasy.

Our complexity as emotional and physical human beings makes relationships difficult and at times impossible. Relationships have limitations. Obviously people cannot be expected to feel a deep interest in nearly every individual whom they meet. Our time is too short and our emotional resources are insufficient for such casual dispersal. Mature people usually have a small number of other persons to whom they devote relatively large amounts of interest and concern. In a family setting, members experience lasting relationships endowed with the strongest love or hate and enjoy their deepest satisfaction or suffer the most painful disappointment. Outside the family circle there will be few intimate friends, for whom the barriers to depth of relationship will be low and the field of relationship extremely large. Peripheral to the close friends, there will probably be individuals with whom we are closely associated in business or in other well-defined common interests, but in other areas only slightly or not at all.

Taken on the literal level, there is probably a good deal of truth in the expression, Good fences make good neighbors; it certainly has psychological implications. There are areas in the lives of most of us that are rightfully opened only to a select few, and areas where no one is permitted. The fact that such areas exist must be accepted, understood, and respected. An awareness of each other's boundaries makes interaction more solid.

The time may come when it is no longer worthwhile to continue a relationship. We all have had the experience of having been close friends with people whom we no longer value, either because we have outgrown them or they us, or because differing experiences and different effects of these experiences have diminished the possibility of continuing a gratifying relationship. If the relationship becomes one of consistent distress or dissatisfaction or boredom, our steadfastness needs to be relinquished. In optimal terms, this change will occur relatively easily by tacit mutual consent. On the other hand, it is generally very painful to us to have to let someone know that we no longer wish to maintain a relationship on the old basis. Sensitivity and tact, as well as forthrightness and strength of purpose, are usually required to sever or radically alter a relationship that has been intense for a long time.

Submissive people may allow a relationship to be lopsided. Such people are not capable of expressing their feelings in a forthright way. They just agree with or placate the other person, giving the impression that the other's behavior does not matter. They are eager to please, never disagreeing no matter what, always wanting the other to approve of them. Having a diminished sense of self-worth, they allow the other to violate their inner space.

The reality of human relationships, especially the interaction of two private worlds, means that we will often not be able to connect with the other person as we ideally desire. We may not be able to immerse ourselves in the other person's perceptions. That is perfectly normal. When we find ourselves directly affected, we should respond courteously, according to how we perceive the situation. When there is a conflict, and every relationship is subjected to conflicts, we may withdraw into a state of cynicism, or we may face the person honestly and openly. Regardless of whether the attitude involves acceptance or confrontation, it will be more productive than submissiveness, which is deadly for the relationship.

In a genuine relationship, each person stands by his or her own perceptions. The reality of these perceptions may be expressed through silent presence and affirmation — that is, through accepting the other person as he or she is, responding with our authentic self and conveying appreciation and regard, thus enabling the person to feel fully human.

Morris West in his celebrated novel *The Shoes of the Fisherman* proclaims the depths of a sound relationship in a pithy paragraph:

> To meet a whole man is an ennobling experience. It costs so much to be a full human being that there are very few who have the enlightenment or the courage to pay the price. One has to abandon altogether the search for security and reach out to embrace the world like a lover, and yet demand no easy return of love. One has to accept pain as a condition of existence. One has to court doubt and darkness as the cost of knowing. One needs a will stubborn in conflict but apt always to the total acceptance of every consequence of living and dying.

Approaching the other person from this position of strength, fully human and humane persons recognize each other for who they are; they say what they mean and mean what they say; they value and contribute to the unfolding of each other without imposing personal perceptions or manipulating each other. This always entails a degree of distance and independence. It does not depend upon one person's revealing to another everything that exists within, but requires only that the person remain who he or she is — being at once an authentic and emotionally responsive self. Martin Buber expresses this value in *The Knowledge of Man*:

> When two men inform one another of their basically different views about an object, each aiming to convince the

other of the rightness of his own way of looking at the matter, everything depends, so far as human life is concerned, on whether each thinks of the other as the one he is, whether each, that is, with all his desire to influence the other, nevertheless unreservedly accepts and confirms him in his being this man and in his being made in this particular way. The strictness and depth of human individuation, the elemental otherness of the other, is then not merely noted as the necessary starting point, but is affirmed from the one being to the other. The desire to influence the other then does not mean the effort to change the other, to inject one's own "righteousness" into him; but it means the effort to let that which is recognized as right, as just, as true through one's influence take seed and grow in the form suited to individuation.

A healthy relationship is not developed and nurtured by reinforcement and habit. It is experienced by being emotionally in touch with one's self and by being emotionally responsive to the other, allowing the inner reality to relate with the inner reality of the other. When someone's presence does really make itself felt, it can be refreshing and rewarding to the other. Then that person responds out of an enhanced sense of self and is prepared to interact creatively. Here awareness meets awareness, a being meets a being, each acknowledging the sacred ground of relationships.

The biggest single gift we can give ourselves during our lifetime does not come in a pretty box or fancy wrappings. It does not cost a lot of money, and it may never impress the neighbors. It is a quiet, readily available commodity known as *self-awareness,* and while it cannot be acquired without an expenditure of time and effort, it will pay off in handsome dividends. *Awareness* of who we are at a given moment, of what experience we are going through, of what our options are, is a most important ingredient that keeps us in charge of the choices that we have at hand or the direction we should take. Growth in a relationship is sometimes a complicated process of personal interaction, requiring an awakening of the forces within and an awareness of subtle nuances outside, as manifested in the words and ways of other people. The secret is to remain genuine, integral to one's own convictions while, at the same time, understanding, tolerating, and respecting the temperament and integrity of other persons.

Thoughts to Ponder

- The origins of conflicts that we experience between ourselves and others are to be found in the fact that too often we do not know what we feel, we do not say what we mean, and we do not do what we say.

- A conflict within blocks progress and cuts off the energy a person needs to grow effectively and connect with others.

- What seems to be missing in your life could actually be the result of a conflict within or an unresolved problem.

- Can you identify the conflict or the unresolved problem and be specific about it? Can you accept that this is the truth about you?

- Can you see your self, the spiritual part of you, as basically good, as desiring to grow and improve and as having a strength that can be brought into action?

- Can you accept that you have negative and positive aspect and that they can be coordinated to produce a change?

Chapter 10

Relating

> For a person to achieve his or her potential there
> must be at least one other person with whom he
> or she is totally open and feels totally safe at the
> same time. We are social beings.
>
> —*Paul Tournier*

One's journey into the self is crucially important. Equally important is *stepping out* of the self and connecting with society, learning to relate with another human being. Your own psyche will tell you how. Just listen to it. However fixed or set in your ways, when you meet another person, *you* become a new being. What you express verbally or nonverbally is real and valid in its own right. It promises growth. Without this momentary contact, we remain frozen in loneliness. Transcending our own world and trusting the experience of the initial contact with another person, we enter a process of something exciting and different. Being willing to meet someone new makes the difference. How do I know that meeting someone new will make a difference? The answer is: You don't know unless you experience it.

Even though many people long for a real friend and have the opportunity to meet somebody, they often have to struggle against the comfort of familiarity. Once you leave familiar surroundings, especially home, for the unknown, you become frightened, particularly of rejection. This scary feeling is often called insecurity or anxiety.

A very important step for us in reaching out to make a contact is to accept our personal insecurity as part of our human condition. We do not need additional muscles, a face lift, a change of color, to be younger or older, to be of the opposite sex, to be superintelligent, or vastly wealthy.

We only need to be human, possessing healthy attitudes and willing to attain new skills. The next step is to accept the other person without the expectation that he or she will agree with us in everything. Even identical twins differ in opinions, lifestyle, and perceptions of the world. Accepting the other person as different from ourselves will establish a strong foundation for a relationship.

"Look not on his countenance, or on the height of his stature," reads a biblical verse. What underlies appearance is the *mutual* desire to reach beyond ourselves. This mutuality cannot be overemphasized. Insecurity is shared, and an invitation to friendship is always welcome.

One of the tasks of successful human relating is to distinguish between the surface and the substance. It is not always easy to separate the apparent from the inherent. People pass judgment on a polished manner, a pleasing face, and a well-chosen wardrobe, each of which is good to possess, but there is more to life and to people than appearances.

The Velveteen Rabbit, a story cast in children's language, tells an adult tale. It records the conversation of discarded toys and their observations about life. They recall the little master who played with them, his pleasures and his illnesses. They remember the rabbits who came out of the woods to sniff them when they were left out overnight. Now they rest in a pile, never used and long forgotten.

"What is real?" asked the rabbit one day when the toys were lying side by side.

"Does it mean having things that buzz inside you and a stick-out handle?"

"Real isn't how you are made," said the Toy Horse. "It's a thing that happens to you when a child loves you for a long time — not just to play with, but really loves you. Then you become real."

"Does it hurt?" asked the rabbit.

"Sometimes," said the Toy Horse, for he was always truthful. "When you are real, you don't mind being hurt."

"Does it happen all at once, like being wound up, or bit by bit?"

"It doesn't happen all at once. You become. It takes a long time. That's why it doesn't happen to people who break easily or who have sharp edges, or have to be carefully kept. Generally, by the time you are *real*, most of your hair has been loved off and your eyes drop out and you get loose at the joints and very shabby. But these things don't matter at all because once you are real, you can't be ugly except to people who don't understand."

Once we have become truly aware of our being, our needs, preferences, and interests, we usually move closer to people or invite people to come closer to us to share and enjoy an experience. This means risking rejection and being turned down once in a while. If we decide not to make the effort to reach out and instead stay at home listening to the stereo or watching television, we are playing a no-win game; not giving ourselves a chance to build a relationship, naturally we experience a sense of emptiness. If we come out of our shell and get involved, our chances of winning — and experiencing a sense of completeness — are raised greatly. Of course it's difficult to make that initial contact, and we may fail, but such a chance is remote.

Considering what relationships mean to us — thinking about the value of interacting with another person, the importance of companionship, of sharing and caring — is helpful. Doing things together, going places, spending time together — all these form the foundation of friendship. Time spent together, emotional availability to each other, and beneficial presence in each other's life make the involvement enjoyable.

People pattern their relationships according to their needs. The important idea to keep in mind is that we all need friends to share experiences, thoughts, ambitions, work, and fun — all of which make life fuller.

We may require a variety of relationships to fill our needs and keep our emotional lives meaningful by enabling us to change and grow. Some people tend to focus so hard on only one special person that they neglect other relationships and end up feeling lonely and frustrated. Expecting one person to fill all our needs is unrealistic and doomed to failure. Many married couples who fall into this trap, feeling that they should relate only to each other, soon find themselves bored and then become resentful when their needs are not being met. We all need other people with whom to socialize, to share hobbies or intimate talk, or simply to join us in going to a play or a movie. No one person can or should be expected to fulfill all our needs.

Having a few good friends who meet our needs and whose needs we are capable of fulfilling enriches our lives and fosters growth far better than would a multitude of superficial relationships. We do not have to restrict ourselves to our own gender; we may choose to relate to people of the opposite sex. Platonic relationships — affectionate relationships without sexual involvement — may be very productive. Opening our minds to this possibility can enhance our lives. Being able to relate to people of either sex broadens the source of relationships, expands our understanding of male/female experiences, and allows us to feel more natural and relaxed. Of course there may be times when the other party involved will want a sexual relationship. Such a decision should be made only by responsible adults who thoroughly understand the consequences of sexual involvement. If a relationship fails for whatever reason, it does not mean that our behavior is the cause; it could be beneficial to try again.

It may be most helpful to us to evaluate our present relationships. Is the path we have been treading satisfactory? We may find that we are maintaining a relationship out of duty, or that we are relating to a role and not to a person, or that our once significant relationship has now soured and that we feel very uncomfortable about it. Individual values change, and the individuals take different directions. We may maintain a relationship at the expense of others — out of nostalgia, lack of motivation, or a feeling of false loyalty. A relationship based on obligation lacks dignity. Such relationships require a great amount of energy and prevent our establishing more relevant, growth-producing relationships. The truth is that most relationships we call friendships are seldom more than mutual-advantage or mutual-exploitation pacts, which dissolve as soon as the element of mutual advantage disappears on either side. When it is no longer emotionally or physically profitable to know each other, we drift apart. Mutual assistance — cooperation — is the basis of social and personal survival, so that any relationship lacking in mutual advantage cannot survive without damage to those who participate.

A real relationship, then, is not one that we have with a person who gives us things or sells us objects at discount prices. A real relationship is one in which we have a warm willingness to participate on a live-and-let-live basis.

Many people feel uncomfortable in social situations. Meeting strangers is difficult for them. They feel inept and do not know what to do. They habitually think, feel, and behave in a passive-receptive way toward the outside world and turn their initiative over to anyone who will pick it up and carry it for them. They live in this world as if they believed it was right for them always to be the guest, never the host. They see nothing unusual or unfair in their habit of abdicating initiative and expecting others to exercise it for their benefit.

In an attempt to relate to others, we unconsciously enter into symbiotic relationships. We make others members of the family, and we treat them — or we expect them to treat us — as siblings. This behavior causes competition and sibling rivalry, inhibiting genuine interaction. We act like children with emerging and perhaps long-repressed infantile needs, expecting others to fulfill them. The role of a child is the role of a guest in the home: everything is done to and for him or her — at least in the beginning. But maturity demands the opposite role of us. Many people have a hard time making the transition into adult behavior. They prefer to remain passive recipients of the good things in life.

Making contact with another person is not a game of impressing, influencing, or winning your point over that person and living happily ever after. It must be an effort to relate with someone directly, honestly, and sympathetically as you share human interests — mutual concerns, joys, and sorrows.

Regardless of how well our egos are integrated, regardless of how restored or intact our self-images are, the moment we come into contact with another human being, we feel some anxiety. This is understandable. Our primitive instincts propel us into a state of momentary fear. We shake hands with one another to reassure ourselves, unconsciously, that there is no weapon in the other's hand. Thus reassured, we feel there is no reason to be afraid. The other person will not hurt us.

A life of solitude may provide an opportunity for contemplation and self-evaluation, for connecting us to our own centers, the inner spring, the soul. Life, however, generally makes more sense as we connect with others, as we touch our fellow human beings. How good it feels to reach out and shake hands with a person whose presence has meaning in our lives. It is a way of maintaining our integrity, of making contact, reflecting, and relating.

When human beings mature, their growth positively affects their environment; it affects their contacts. Human beings affect people around them, and they are urged toward their growth. Your personal growth should not offend people around you or cause them to wither; instead, it should cause them to burgeon. Positive behavior and personal growth are inspiring. I find that the more I mature and feel self-reliant, the better that maturity and self-reliance are for fostering my relationships. Learning the art of relating to others helps us to nurture our growing self-esteem and strengthens our relationships with ourselves and others. This kind of learning promises a more productive life. However, it takes patience, persistence, and perseverance.

Larry gave the impression of being fortunate. But such an impression was misleading. I saw him surrounded by a crowd at one of his elegant parties. Being surrounded by people is, of course, not necessarily proof of having good relationships. He possessed power, fame, and material wealth. Yet he was a lonely man. He smoked a big cigar, anesthetizing himself as he walked lost and lonely among his guests. He was unavailable for personal contact.

Lynn was more pathetic than lonely Larry. She managed to live year after year with minimal contact with others. In the morning, she went to her job; in the evening, she returned home; she had supper alone, and then read or watched television. Each day followed a similar pattern. On the weekend, she drove to the shore or visited a museum, always alone. She had a variety of excuses for not making any contacts: "I like my solitude. I have never found anyone I really cared about. I don't want to get involved. It's too much trouble." Avoiding contact with others was safer than risking a possible rejection or a temporary acceptance.

The stronger we feel within ourselves, the more complete is the contact with others. The weak person has limited choices. He or she can be in contact only with weak or weaker people. The loved and lovable person who values selfhood chooses people with healthy self-esteem. Having a network of relationships gives us a sense of belonging and makes it possible to satisfy our emotional needs. Contact with another person helps us to know and accept who we are and to overcome loneliness and alienation. As human beings, we are social animals; we need to form relationships with others. That is how we share our human dilemma and add meaning to our lives.

Academic courses are so diverse that they cover almost everything in the universe. Name a subject, and someone will know where to go to get the information. Yet, if you find it difficult to relate with others, there is a scarcity of courses to train you effectively. Fortunately, in recent years, seminars in communication skills are being conducted, therapeutic groups can be found, and many self-improvement books have been published. It is up to each of us to start our self-reconstruction. If we are to connect with others or to establish relationships, we must start the connection within.

If we say to a friend, "We must create a relationship," the friend will laugh at us. "A relationship! What are you talking about?"

A relationship is not a miracle that just happens, or something that simply occurs between two people and stands forever. If you have had or if you now have friends, you will realize it took time, effort, and ability to give to them and share with them. This relationship was created by availability, emotional and physical presence, awareness of who you are and who the other person is. It took talking, investment of time, struggling with crises, dealing with differences, and coming to grips with each other's reality.

Saint-Exupery used the simple form of a children's tale in *The Little Prince* to convey the deepest truths we know about relationships. He tells the story of a prince who comes to earth from an asteroid. While living on the asteroid, the Little Prince has a flower for company, and he expends a great deal of effort caring for it. His flower tells him that she is the only one of her kind in the universe. On earth, he discovers a garden containing thousands of roses exactly like her. He meets the fox. The encounter and the ensuing conversation with the fox is truly a rediscovery of our human dilemma as we decide to make contact with another person.

"Good morning," said the fox.

"Good morning," the Little Prince responded politely, although when he turned around he saw nothing.

"I am right here," the voice said, "under the apple tree."

"Who are you?" asked the Little Prince, and added, "You are very pretty to look at."

"I am a fox," the fox said.

"Come and play with me," proposed the Little Prince. "I am so unhappy."

"I cannot play with you," the fox said. "I am not tamed."

"Ah! Please excuse me," said the Little Prince. But after some thought, he added, "But what does that mean — 'tame'?"

"You do not live here," said the fox. "What is it that you are looking for?"

"I am looking for men," said the Little Prince. "What does that mean — 'tame'?"

"Men," said the fox. "They have guns, and they hurt. It is very disturbing. They also raise chickens. These are their only interests. Are you looking for chickens?"

"No," said the Little Prince. "I am looking for friends. What does that mean — 'tame'?"

As the tale unfolds, *ties* are established, the Little Prince understands what the word "tame" means, and a beautiful friendship develops. The wise fox reserves a promised secret until departure time.

"Goodbye," said the Little Prince.

"Goodbye," said the fox. "And now here is my secret, a very simple secret: It is only with the heart that one can see rightly; what is essential is invisible to the eye."

Pick any part of the story and carefully read it over. You will rediscover areas that resemble aspects of your life each time you attempted to reach out to somebody.

Appearances and positions in life are not important: one is a fox and the other is a prince. Both need each other, but it is difficult because the fox is not tame and the prince does not know what "tame" means. Think of the verb "to tame." The taming process makes friendship possible because, through it, the uniqueness of a person becomes evident and gives meaning to a relationship. The value of a person is not identified in terms of stature, skill, or appearance. Friendship, in a poetic portrait, is a facet of love demonstrated in caring for the needs of others. It allows a feeling of responsibility to surface when one tames the other. Before the taming process takes place, no activity or movement is possible. To tame is to remove the barrier of fear of both animals and humans. Tamers must prove themselves harmless. Once the taming occurs, we become caring and loving for what we tame. Afterward, we understand what we tamed.

In our terms, taming another human being need not be an authoritarian process. In the sense of the Little Prince, taming does not mean to make docile or tractable or to tone down and soften, as happens so often when one individual stands out strongly and threatens the shaky existence of the other. To tame individuals implies establishing warm ties with them. This means a willingness to enter into their world and to respect their unique requirements. To enter their world does not mean invading their privacy or controlling the relationship. To tame means not being in a hurry and being willing to come to the meaning and value of friendship by just being with the person. "Men have forgotten this truth," said the fox. "But you must not forget it. You become responsible, forever, for what you have tamed."

To tame means to earn the trust and confidence of another. As a by-product, one gains credibility, and this cannot be betrayed without damaging one's integrity. That is why relationships are major responsibilities.

I recall an intimate encounter with a great spiritual figure, Athenagoras I, patriarch of Constantinople. "When I was a priest in a small village in Greece," he said, "every evening a number of peasants would pass by my house to see me. These simple folk used to say to me, 'I came that we may look at each other.' In their eyes I saw the miracle that is to be human — I saw God."

The old patriarch had discovered that intellectual dialogues tend to confuse people. It takes the simplicity of the peasant and the acceptance of the patriarch and the faith of both to start a genuine and productive relationship.

Thoughts to Ponder

- Sometimes it is difficult to know who you are; yet, other voices are always available and ready to define who you are. You can reach out and find a friend with whom you can interact honestly and warmly; such interaction will give you a new dimension about yourself.

- When you begin to share the inner regions of yourself, when you divulge your deepest feelings, convictions, and experiences, then you have already offered true and vital dimensions of yourself.

- There is an indelible reality in human relations. Each person lives in a private world, and it is difficult to immerse ourselves in that person's perceptions, unless that person makes it possible. We need to be careful with the sensitive areas.

- When we are in conflict with the other, it is better to withdraw with the understanding that the other person is entitled to his or her convictions. Genuine interaction will continue when we state how we feel about the conflicting issue; we can express the opposite view without coercing the other person to agree with us.

- Growth of the self requires a loving encounter in which each person recognizes the other as he or she is; each says what he or she means and means what is said; each values and contributes to the unfolding of the other without imposing or manipulating. Growth implies some degree of distance and independence. It does not mean a total fusion of two personalities into one.

- Growth of the relationship does not depend upon one revealing to the other everything that exists within; it requires only that the person be who he or she is and be genuinely present.

Chapter 11

The Oldest Form of Therapy

> Real friendship is a kind of divine act that
> enables two people to share feelings that life
> denies them continually. It requires all your belief
> in the possibility that you can walk on water
> with somebody because of the sheer electrical
> discharge of love.
>
> —*Stuart Miller*

When humans initially became conscious of their joy and suffering, they sought camaraderie and comfort in the company of other humans. In sharing their common fate with each other, they became aware of a good feeling that surfaced and did what they could to maintain this bonding, known as friendship.

History has preserved some examples of friendship where people risked their lives to save a friend. "Greater love has no man than the one who lays down his life for his friends," claimed the Teacher of teachers. And he did sacrifice his life for his friends.

When Jesus said to his disciples, "Love one another," it was not so much an emotional attachment that he was referring to. He was referring to the bonds between them due to the thoughts, the life, and habits they shared. He commanded them to transform these bonds into *friendship*, so that they would not be allowed to turn into impure attachment and hatred.

As in the past, many people today, instead of running to a psychotherapist's office, seek out the company of friends, at least one friend, whom they can trust, to solicit some solace.

There is a great feeling of relief to be experienced in the presence of a good friend, especially when reciprocity is present.

In speaking of *friendship* as an alternative to therapy, two areas need to be clarified. First, when people learn to do helpful things with each other, genuine friendship will facilitate the healing process immensely. It is a mistake to call connections and acquaintances friends. We have few friendships, because we are not willing to pay the price of friendship, which is time, commitment, caring, and sharing, at the risk of exposing our own vulnerability. Second, if and when psychopathology is present, it is better to seek the therapist trained in specific skills.

Unlike acquaintances, friendships are a form of unwritten contract. As with a contract, friends enter into a usually unspoken agreement that they will in the future react toward each other in certain generally specified ways. They will be pleased to see each other; they will support each other when either is threatened; they will be available for discussions; they will be truthful and honest as they interact; they will publicly admit their friendship; they will have each other's best interests at heart; they will attempt to share each other's joy and sorrow; above all, they will be predictable and loyal within the confines of the friendship.

Friendship needs delicate handling. We can ruin it by unwitting blundering at its very birth, and we can kill it by neglect. It is not every flower that has vitality enough to grow in stony ground. Lack of reticence, which is only the outward sign of lack of respect, is responsible for the death of many potentially good friendships.

The method for the development of friendship finds its best and briefest summary in the Golden Rule. To do to, and for, your friend what you would have your friend do to, and for, you, is a simple compendium of the whole duty of friendship. Friendship is a gradual process. We tell our friends a little about ourselves, and they give us information about themselves. It is a two-way street of give and take. The actual information is of subsidiary significance, but what is vital for the construction of a good friendship is the style, manner, and generosity with which it is offered and received.

The very first principle of friendship is that it is mutual, as among spiritual equals, and it claims reciprocity, mutual confidence, and faithfulness. There must be empathy and sympathy to keep in touch with each other, but sympathy and empathy need to be constantly exercised. It is a channel of communication that has to be kept open, or it will soon be clogged and closed. Practicing sympathy and empathy implies an effort to cultivate similar interests with a potential friend, although that comes naturally as a result of fellowship. This process of developing common interests does not mean absorption of one of the partners or the identity of both.

It is fascinating to see that there are friendships based on differences. A difference may charm and educate a person. Sameness may cause boredom. When a friend is different from you in likes and dislikes, goals, aspirations, and personality traits, it is good to observe the differences without judgment. You may learn and grow from your contact with that person. Part of the challenge and charm of interaction lies in the differences. Good friends agree to disagree. What is essential is that there is a real desire and a genuine effort to understand each other. It is well worthwhile to take pains to preserve a relationship so full of bliss for both. Here, especially, when in search of a good friend, there is a strong need for patience. When we notice in a friend things that detract from that person's worth, or things that irritate us, tenderness and patience are needed. The commitment is not to an individual but to the ideal of tolerance. Focusing on such an ideal, people experience wonderful delights.

There is good in every person. Well-meaning friends will seek out these hidden strengths, which may be temporarily dormant, but are alive and well, waiting to be used. A bit of confidence mixed with optimism encourages us in the belief that we are able to improve our lot. Pessimistic talk about personal inadequacies, ill fate, and the wrongs and injustices of life can be listened to once and then put in the bottom drawer, not to be opened. Negativity and pessimism need to be broken in the most gentle way possible. If we are not careful, misery and despair can become a way of life.

Of course, we need to be sensitive in times when intense sorrow or a feeling of worthlessness, failure, or low self-esteem is evident. Critical situations require support and sympathy, and the truly concerned friend must adopt a tough stance to combat the negativism that can be present in crises.

Two friends were traveling together through a forest when

a bear rushed out upon them. One of the travelers happened to be in front, and he seized the branch of a tree, climbed high, and hid himself among the leaves. The other, seeing no help available, threw himself flat upon the ground with his face in the dust. The bear, coming up to him, put his muzzle close to his ear and sniffed and sniffed. At last with a growl he shook his head and slouched off, for bears will not touch dead meat. Then the friend in the tree came down to his comrade, and laughing, said, "What was it that Master Bruin whispered to you?"

"He told me," said the other, 'Never trust a friend who deserts you in a pinch.'"

The fable is a good reminder that friendship becomes evident at the time of need.

Accept your friend with his flaws, claims an old adage. It may be that in the course of interaction, our friend's virtues may transcend the flaws. And it may be foolish to be irritated at a few blemishes, forgetting our own.

Trust is another prerequisite for making a friend. If we are suspicious or argumentative, it will be difficult to make a friend. Suspicion kills friendship. An openness of mind, before friendship can be formed, is a better approach. We must give of self freely and unreservedly. The warm nature that acts on impulse may be more effective than the overcautious nature that is afraid to commit itself. It is a fact of life that we cannot do anything with each other without a certain amount of trust.

We can certainly close our eyes to the faults of others and open them to our own. One fine day two crabs came out of their sea-home to take a stroll on the sand. "Child," said the mother, "you are walking very ungracefully. You should accustom yourself to walking straight forward without twisting from side to side."

"Pray, mother," said the young one, "do but set the example yourself, and I will follow you."

Knowing that all humans stumble now and then and that the one who never makes a mistake never accomplishes anything, we can learn to be tolerant and forgiving. When we sense that we are treading on sensitive areas, we can be sure that someone is hurting. Why not use a dash of compassion, which is the antitoxin of the soul. Where there is compassion, even the most poisonous impulses remain relatively harmless. The cultivation of friendship largely depends on our ability to foster a capacity for compassion. Some well-educated people are not as compassionate as the uneducated. "The hardness of heart of the educated worries me," said an old timer.

After trust comes *faithfulness*. It is another prerequisite to the maintaining of friendship. The way to have a friend is to be a friend. To be a friend, we must be a friend to ourselves, by being true to our highest and best attributes and by aligning ourselves with the enduring values of human life that make for growth and progress. For most of us, life is made up of little things, and many a friendship withers through sheer neglect. Hearts are alienated, because each is waiting for some great occasion for displaying affection. The great spiritual value of friendship lies in the opportunities it affords for service, and if these are neglected it is only to be expected that the gift will fade out. Friendship, which begins with sentiment, will not live and thrive on sentiment. There must be loyalty, which finds expression in service. We must be ready to lay hold of every opportunity of serving our friend. It is not the greatness of the help or the intrinsic value of the gift of friendship that gives it its worth, but the evidence it gives of care, love, and thoughtfulness. Such thoughtfulness keeps our sentiment in evidence to both parties. If we never show our kind feeling, what guarantee has our friend that it exists? Faithfulness is truly the outward sign of a vigilant soul. If there is a person that you have been drawn to, it is worthwhile being loyal and true to that attraction. Then you may have an opportunity to see the inherent goodness and potential greatness in the other.

Friendship with ulterior motives or selfish purposes cannot last long. If its purpose lies in personal interests, one of the persons involved is being set up for disappointment. If you expect a friend to serve your interests, you are developing a potential enemy. To sacrifice a friend for personal advantage of gain or position is to deprive our self of the capacity for friendship.

In your lifetime, you must have met people who crave new experiences, new friends. In this matter of friendship they are ready to forsake the old for the new. They are always finding a swan in every goose they meet. Such passion for novelty is short-lived. A poem reminds us:

> Make new friends, but keep the old;
> Those are silver, these are gold.

What really keeps the fabric of friendship solid and colorful is a touch of spirituality. Friendship cannot become permanent unless it becomes spiritual. There must be fellowship in the deepest parts of the soul, community in the highest thoughts, camaraderie in the noblest actions, sympathy with the best endeavors.

Friendship is not a luxury; it is a spiritual opportunity. In its process of development we grow in grace, we learn to love and to care, we learn to receive and to give.

Above all, when we have brought out the best, what is highest and deepest in human nature, we experience *healing*.

To be a strong hand in the dark to another in time of need, to be a cup of strength to quench the thirst of a human being in a crisis of weakness, is to know the glory of life.

Thoughts to Ponder

- If someone is seeking our help, we really cannot pose as experts who are in a position to dispense wisdom and "know-how" to somebody who does not possess it. Acting as a human being rather than as an expert exhibits a genuine willingness to help others.

- When we are approached by someone in trouble, we can bear in mind that at another time, in another place, we may experience similar difficulties. Our response and reaction to a person in need ought to reflect this possibility.

- A doctor or a therapist may be keenly aware of what is the nature of illness. One may prescribe medicine, while the other may apply psychotherapeutic skills. However, do either possess superior knowledge of *how life should be lived* by virtue of their profession?

- Aside from our psychological perceptions, we can rely on friendship to provide us with knowledge about the individual we wish to help.

- In an effort to emphasize the equality of our relationship with an individual in trouble, we should not be afraid to reveal our own vulnerabilities.

- We have found a friend when we feel comfortable in expressing our own views, in disagreeing, in praising, in giving and receiving advice. Seeing another's strengths and sincerely praising them is a sign of genuine friendship. Sensing another's weaknesses, we must be careful and sensitive as to *how* we point them out.

• A good friend could give you more joy than a big bank account. Give quality time to your friendship and you will receive wonderful dividends.

Chapter 12

In Search of Uniqueness

> We assert our uniqueness best by recognizing
> that of others. It is not enough merely to respect
> another's uniqueness — we must defend it, even
> against ourselves.
>
> —*Herbert Holt*

You could search the whole world and fail to find one human being who is your exact physical counterpart; even if you are an identical twin, there will be disparities. One of the twins is usually a little bigger, stronger, quicker, even smarter than the other. No two children in the same family, under the same roof, from the same parents grow up to be identical.

If our personal physical characteristics are unique, what can we say about our intellect, our emotions, and our capabilities, the unfathomed mysteries of our psyche? Certainly it is true that each one of us is individual, unique. The point is, how far do we want to push this uniqueness? How individualized does each of us want or need to be?

Several decades ago, Carl Gustav Jung first made the individual the center of his therapy. He coined the term "individuation." Later, Abraham Maslow and Carl Rogers, independently, took the same direction with the concept of "self-actualization." Since then, inquirers who are in therapy or who attend encounter groups are, presumably, in search of their own unique identity.

Is there such a quality as uniqueness? Who is unique? Do we want to be unique? How much of a unique individual do we want to be? How different from our fellows do we wish to be? Does anyone of us really want to be a completely separate individual?

The majority of people are content to go along with the flow. Most people accept their place in life and go quietly about their business. Today, the blue-collar and white-collar workers, the unemployed or the unemployable on welfare, the service and sales persons, middle and top management, teachers, doctors, lawyers, architects, and even psychologists follow identical patterns as members of the service class.

However, all the members of the above categories, in their own unique ways, are in search of an identity. We struggle with the illusion and sometimes with the reality of upward mobility, through education and hard work, through cunning and manipulation, and we manage to exchange one pattern of life for another. We exchange the label we inherit from our parents for the label of the man or woman on the next step of the socio-economic ladder; we move from a small house to a bigger one in a more expensive suburb, from a smaller to a bigger car, from a creative church group to an exclusive country club.

The person who reaches fame and fortune may feel unique. We want to know how he made it. What methods did she employ? What is the gain? What is the cost?

At the age of thirty-eight, Joel became a partner in a law firm where he earned from $250,000 to $300,000 a year. His name, printed in gold letters, was mounted on the sign at the entrance, a tribute to his success.

He pursued further investments in real estate, worked hard all day, and brought his attaché case home on weekends. He had little time for his family. Work was his priority. Truly, he earned his success but, understandably, his home life suffered.

In an effort to restore his shattered situation at home, one day he approached his wife, Linda, for some romantic time.

She seized the opportunity. "I'm not a sexual service station, nor am I a wailing wall where you can come and cry about how hard you work."

"What am I?" he fired back. "Some kind of money-making machine to gratify all your expensive tastes?"

Joel and Linda responded to each other with repressed irritation and accumulated anger. They did not know how to do otherwise. The ongoing unverbalized feelings, their starving for love and attention caused them to give each other grief. Frustrated in their wedlocked relationship and avoiding discussion of their sterile co-existence, they blamed each other for lack of caring and for undefined missing things in their life. Angrily, they pointed fingers at each other in their effort to prove the other wrong. A long hour later, the emotions subsided.

The angry outburst resulted in a sensible dialogue. They stayed up most of the night, articulating feelings and perceptions of each other. They loved each other deeply and they loved their eight-year-old son and six-year-old daughter.

In the week that followed, Joel resigned from the firm and joined a lawyer friend in a smaller office. To supplement his income, which was about a quarter of what it had been, he sold his real estate and his expensive boat; he no longer attended public-relations dinners; he gave up his country club activities and settled down to be a husband and father and enjoy his family.

Joel was a loving man. He was glad he had abandoned the rat race of success. However, when the family went on their second Saturday outing together, Joel was horrified to find that he was bored to death and thought with pleasure of his return to his office on Monday. Was it a mistake to have given up his position in the prestigious firm?

He developed a nagging ulcer. With tears in his eyes, he described his situation to me. Domestic life irritated him. His children constantly demanded attention. Had he made an irreparable mistake? Had he sacrificed the strenuous life he knew and enjoyed for a simple, shared family life that could not satisfy him?

The situation is common enough. People come to a point in their lives, at thirty-eight, forty, or even in the late fifties, when they realize they are not living their own unique, authentic lives. They suffer as Joel did. They feel the panic he felt. Giving scares them. They do not know how to make a different life. Some refuse to take personal initiative to pursue other interests.

Joel cherished his success; he did what he wanted to do; he traveled, bought any commodities he felt he needed, and pursued new experiences in partying and attending conferences.

An attractive woman, a medical doctor with a lawsuit against her, sought Joel's help. He represented her most effectively in court and won the case. Along with his handsome fee came a passionate affair that revolutionized his life. The doctor was eight years younger than he and more attractive than his wife; however, he did not realize that she had a hidden agenda. Having dated many men, she had stopped viewing them as a measure of her popularity and began to ask herself what sort of husband and father each of them might be. Seeing Joel's dedication to his work and his emotional availability to her, she visualized what sort of home and family she would have with him.

When he told her that he did not plan to leave his wife, she fainted. He was scared and felt guilty. He made up his mind to put her out of his life. That was not an easy task, for he found himself deeply in love and unable to let her go. Being a man of his caliber, he thought he could handle his situation. Every problem has a solution, and he was determined to find a viable one. He became a *new man*, the ambitious attorney who had all he wanted. Having a mistress was not a crime as long as you did not hurt anyone, he rationalized. At his office, he manifested eagerness to get along well with others. He tried to organize his private life at home in accordance with the requirements of large organizations. He made efforts to sell himself as if his own personality were a commodity with an assignable market value. But his neurotic need for affection, reassurance, and physical gratification led him to seek involvement in other extramarital affairs. However, the corruptibility of his values triggered guilt feelings. His doctor mistress began to make increasing claims on his life. She demanded exclusivity. Joel emphasized his need for time to evaluate his situation. He felt stressed and terribly unhappy. He developed colitis. "Slow down. Take time out," suggested his physician.

Therapy sessions revealed that Joel had lost part of his humanity during the years of his cold-blooded, competitive struggle to succeed. He realized it was not his own life, his unique life, he was living, but a life of fantasy — and not even his own fantasy. You may have witnessed this type of behavior in parents who try to live out their own fantasies through the life of the child. In Joel's case, the brilliant career was the idea of his mother, a woman who had inundated his childhood with dreams of luxury and financial independence in the great world, but whose actual experience as an adult was most limited.

Joel was overwhelmed by his own childhood deprivations and the frustrations of being trapped in the powerless confines of a dysfunctional family where his father, an alcoholic, was demanding and punitive and the mother emotionally disturbed. Home life was built on a constant undercurrent of tension, anxiety, and worry. He kept hoping that everything would be fine, but he was not sure that would be the case. Occasionally his reality gave way to fantasies of grandiosity. He embraced a magnanimous idea: one day he would be a judge, and then people would respect him. He was looking forward to the day of his liberation, but he had a few more years of tyranny to endure at home.

Joel indulged in the fantasy that all was normal in his family, although he did not know what *normal* entailed. He lied when it was just as easy to tell the truth, he judged himself without mercy, he had difficulty in making friends or having fun, he overreacted to changes over which he had no control, and he constantly sought approval. He felt that he was different from other children.

Now as an adult in a new job, he felt uncomfortable having to do things that in larger firms are assigned to specialists. Faced with more energy and less turmoil, he felt overwhelmed at the prospect of being free to decide what to do with his life now. He described the many situational decisions he expected therapy to help him make.

"It's hard being all grown-up and mature," I said.

"Now that I have many choices, it's hard for me to decide on my own," he replied.

"And you want me to tell you what to do."

"You don't do that, do you?"

"I have enough trouble looking after myself. It's hard enough deciding how to run my own life without trying to figure out what's best for someone else."

"And I'm paying all this money, for what?"

"I don't know." I smiled.

Therapy helps clients to become more conscious of how they do run their lives. In that way they may come to understand what they get out of living as they do, and at what costs. Therapy as a guided self-inventory is likely to increase their awareness of options, from which they may make an actual choice.

Joel's therapy centered on his longing to be taken care of, his desire that others would honor his wishes and respect him.

His feelings were explored in a way that allowed him to experience the anguished vulnerability and poignant sadness that underlay his willfully insistent wish for uninterrupted happiness. Gradually his therapy shifted to his heightening awareness of his self-defeating, superficial lifestyle and to his search for uniqueness.

It was painfully difficult for him to begin to accept his adult life as it really was. Each time he clearly faced yet another hidden aspect of his insistence that he should be treated as someone special, he would experience more anguish and vulnerability of having to live the rest of his life without compensation for having missed loving care so desperately when he was a child.

The core reactions to that deprivation were rage, grief, and helplessness.

Joel's recovery was slow. About a year later, he had found more points of shared interest with his family. From occasional walks to playing tennis with his wife, he grew to cherish her company, and they spent time together for the pure joy of being with each other. On Friday evenings, Joel took his daughter to her dancing lessons and enjoyed watching her learning the steps. The family usually spent Saturdays swimming at the local Y, followed by dinner at a restaurant. Camping in July became an annual experience to which they all looked forward.

The once aggressive, ambitious attorney learned to enjoy himself, and through his children he recaptured lost time in his youth.

We are all born with a genetic endowment to make a life plan for ourselves. The spark of God in each person spurs us to take for ourselves as much as we can grasp. If we become greedy in the process, nothing in the world will satisfy us, for there is no such thing as *enough* in life. From the day we are born, we are shaping a life plan. From our parents or parenting adults, our environment, our society, teachers, and peers, we take what is available to shape our plan.

It is a sacred and secret plan, uniquely ours. It has nothing at all to do with conscious decision or conscious choice. A conscious choice can take only a very small, narrow part of our lives into consideration, because we are evolving humans with limited perceptions, and like a camera lens, we take in only what we see and understand with our conscious mind. But this deeper plan takes all into consideration and reveals itself as we mature. It is made out of the whole self, the needs and demands and capabilities, the potentiality of the whole person. Regardless of what part of our planet we occupy, this plan is part of our human potential.

Of course, a child's environment can stifle or distort, even destroy, the intended authentic life for which that child is uniquely born. Children growing up in Africa or India or China are subjected to great deprivation, and although they may survive and adjust to the place of birth, who can say whether or not they fulfill their potential, authentic selves?

What I find truly inspiring in countries that we consider less fortunate is the spirit of the people. Downtrodden people who suffer deprivation have a plan for their existence. When I traveled as a missionary, not as a tourist, in the Middle East, in parts of Asia Minor, and in Africa, I looked into people's eyes and discovered a warmth, a spirit of acceptance, an inner beauty. I saw some of them as closer to life's mystery than many of us who luxuriate in the abundance of American life. Indeed, they gave me more than I gave them.

In our American environment, the strong influence of parents, or the lack of it, or peer pressure can turn a child aside into an unauthentic life. Many people who select the goals of wealth, success, and prestige discover sometime in their lives that their choice does not bring them the satisfaction it promised, that it does not meet their inner needs and desires. They experience a feeling of emptiness. Can they find any other direction in life?

To examine and recreate a life is a difficult and necessary task. To make the task easier, we should look at ourselves every day for just a little while. If we postpone the task for too long, it becomes very difficult indeed.

The gravest mistake we make is in setting for ourselves a course that is so narrow that it cuts us off from all relationships except functional ones. In such a course, we choose to have no family, no friends, no one with whom to share our joy and sorrow, and no one against whose values we could measure our own and, perhaps, come to question. Knowing no one else, we can never know ourselves. Ignorance of self leads to disaster.

A great deal can be said in favor of people who try for a life of the intellect or of adventure and novelty, or simply a life of living and loving and enjoying what is available each day:

making friends, establishing significant relationships in marriage or otherwise, choosing to have children or not. Life is to be cherished. People should take time to smell the flowers, eat a balanced meal, even if it is not elaborate, care about other human beings and have them care in return. This does not mean people should not have some fame and fortune. The question is: Does one have to be rich or successful or famous to live a good life as a human being? The answer has always been clear to people in all times and in all societies.

Thoughts to Ponder

- Observing our own gullibility, we may protect ourselves from falling into fantasies that can seriously influence our uniqueness.

- A person can be mature and into middle years and still feel a sense of inadequacy when faced with societal pressures.

- It is a liberating experience to realize that we cannot influence many people, that our concept of truth and our personal values are totally subjective and not significant to other people.

- Clinging to our fantasy of uniqueness is a way of denying realization of just how limited we are. As we outgrow the prolonged years of childhood, we are confronted with the overwhelming realities of grown-up life and our ability to respond responsibly.

- To go on maturing, increasing our potential for fulfillment and happiness in the world as it is, each of us must go through repeated losses of naive fantasies. The threshold of each new stage of life involves hard work. With each step forward, we take two steps backward.

- Perhaps *wisdom* is no more than patience and acceptance of what we cannot change, sharing what life provides, and being grateful for being alive.

- Sometimes we cannot perceive that there are more personal options and that it is all right for us to choose them in place of what society's standards have taught us is "the right way."

- There are people who will do almost anything to impress others with their *uniqueness*. They dramatize their situations, seeing their particular roles as special, attempt heroic actions, and pursue positions of glory. However, these speculated fantasies are interrupted by the reality that their stay is short, their position vulnerable, and their impact upon others minimal.

Chapter 13

I Feel, Therefore I Am

One day you feel good and the next day you feel
bad, and between those two poles are compressed
all the joys of heaven and the anguish of hell.

—*Willard Gaylin*

Feelings and emotions are two sides of the same coin. In the last
thirty years, people have been exploring *inner space* conditions,
seeking various therapeutic modalities to find answers to their
chronic dissatisfaction with life. Feelings have become the focal
point of their therapy, expressing them has become the task, and
some sort of resolution has become the goal.

Feelings imply the power or faculty of experiencing a physical sensation, an awareness that usually connotes absence of
reasoning. *Emotions* imply an intense feeling with physical as
well as mental manifestations: temples throbbing, eyes dilating,
heart beating faster as a result of fear or joy. There is absolutely
no way to prove that feelings exist. Feelings have no visible substance. Whatever shape they have is elusive and changeable. Yet
they are very real and pervade our lives. We experience them,
sometimes with palpable intensity. We may try to avoid them,
we may ignore them, we may suppress them, we may cope
with them, we may rationalize them, but whatever we do, they
accompany us constantly. Many people find them a nuisance.
"Feelings get in the way," one business executive complained to
me. "If I could eliminate them, I'd be able to be more objective
and do my job better."

"Show me an emotion or feeling," a radical behaviorist once
challenged me. "If you can lay it on the table for me to look at,

maybe I'll believe in it." Obviously I had failed to convince him that feelings exist. Equally obvious is that my failure to lay it on the table proved nothing. Had he demanded to see a thought, an idea — justice, freedom, love — it would have been just as absurd. It would have led to the conclusion that ideas, likewise, are nonexistent.

Clearly, most people not only believe that feelings exist, but they recognize the power that feelings convey and would like to be in charge of them — to keep the positive ones and weed out the negative. The metaphor is apt: negative feelings, like weeds, spring up unwanted, flourish at the expense of growing things, and should be uprooted as early as possible. The old song has the right idea: "You gotta accentuate the positive, eliminate the negative."

You may remember the exchange between a man and his wife in a recent film:

SHE: Look, I have feelings.

HE: Let me tell you about feelings. I've done a lot of research on feelings. When you discover them, bury them — fast.

We all know from experience that negative feelings cannot be pushed aside in the hope that they will fade away. They need to be understood, identified, confronted, worked through, for otherwise they will fester and spawn problems. When we try to ignore the feeling, we are also ignoring the problem that generated it. But it merely submerges, and we are left trying to deal with superficial symptoms, which are often confusing and misleading.

It is useful here to distinguish between emotions (anger, fear, embarrassment, and so forth) and bodily sensations (pains, itches, tickles, tingles), although at least one school of thought maintains that all feelings are bodily. I find this hard to accept. The localized physical pain in my big toe is different from the generalized anger that I feel because you stepped on it carelessly. Often a direct relationship exists between emotions and the body, but only in the sense that the body *expresses* feelings. My fear, for example, is expressed in involuntary trembling. Repressed rage sometimes induces a convulsive stiffness of the body. On the other hand, to suggest that the body expresses a pain or an itch makes little sense. Such responses are physical in both origin and response.

A more compelling reason for drawing such a distinction between feelings and bodily sensations becomes obvious when we begin to talk about *interpersonal* feelings, which are susceptible to directedness. While it is conceivable that I might experience a tight feeling in the pit of my stomach or in my head *because of* someone, it seems more reasonable to suggest that the tight sensation is my body's way of expressing something much deeper and, indeed, expressing it very inadequately.

We still have great difficulty distinguishing between feeling and thinking. In everyday life we are hardly aware of the way we blur the line between them. Here is an example:

CHARLES *(to Cindy):* I'm a little reluctant to say this to you, but one thing that really bothers me about you is that you talk too much; what you say is never that interesting and you constantly interrupt when people are talking.

COUNSELOR: *(to Cindy):* What are you feeling?

CINDY: I feel he's right.

Observation: Cindy really means, "I think that he's right."

It is a common tendency to use the term "feel" in place of "think." In other words, most sentences that begin with "I feel," rarely end up as a statement about a feeling. The pronoun "that" is the tip-off and indicates what will follow will be actually a statement about a thought or an opinion, not a feeling as such.

In our example, Cindy certainly must have had some feelings, doubtless very strong ones. Who wouldn't, after such a verbal attack? Being forced to answer what the feelings are, Cindy takes refuge in a weak generality rather than face the prospect, probably painful, of discovering and then acknowledging what her feelings are. Feelings often get tramped down this way — the technical term is "repression" — although often as not, unconsciously, and that is precisely the point. Many people are not in close touch with their feelings.

Let's consider a less dramatic and more ordinary situation. You encounter someone in the normal course of events, in socializing or working. Within the first minute you react at some level with three or four or more different feelings. You may not be aware of them, you may not be in contact with them, but they have been generated, and they are there. Invariably, people say, "How can I possibly have any feelings about this person? I've just met him." But you can, and you do. Although you may not recognize these feelings or identify them, they, nevertheless, *program* your responses, in some fashion, to this person.

Feelings resemble icebergs: only the tip is perceptible; the ominous and potentially dangerous bulk is submerged. One such iceberg is fear. The upper tip, the small part we are conscious of, may be experienced as a vague discomfort or dislike, a slight tendency to hesitate or avoid, a reluctance or shyness. Just below the surface, the following state might be reported: "I feel anxious." At a deeper level, someone might admit, "I'm scared." Deeper yet lies the feeling of sheer panic.

The visible part of the iceberg, with anger, for example, appears in threatening forms such as teasing, sarcasm, humor, disparagement — the controlled tendency to be judgmental, critical, disdainful. At successively deeper levels lie annoyance, irritation, anger, pure rage.

When someone says, "It's not that I'm angry with you, it's just that I'm so disappointed in you," you may be quite sure this is merely an attenuated expression of anger, but one that leaves the angry party relatively free of risk. Another way to express anger is rage; but that leaves the angry person vulnerable to criticism for being childish and immature.

Love, hurt, guilt, and many other feelings also occur in the shape of icebergs. One of the more interesting features of the iceberg phenomenon is that, above the surface, feelings readily turn into impulses, and the impulses are usually acted upon. To put it another way, persons with considerable submerged guilt tend to deal experientially with only a small part of it; their outward behavior may involve a lot of explaining or a vaguely defensive posture while, in reality, they are thoroughly out of touch with their true feelings since they lie so deep. The behavior is so tenuously related to these submerged feelings that it may seem totally incongruous and contradictory. Out of touch with our feelings, we tend toward programmed actions and reactions, largely mechanical and predictable, because we are unconsciously masking what lurks below the surface.

We need not go very far to discover the reason most of us are out of touch with our feelings. Our conditioning began very,

very early. Feelings, overtly and honestly expressed, made our parents uncomfortable, so they taught us things such as the following:

- Big boys don't cry.

- Girls don't use bad words.

- You don't really hate your little sister, do you?

- You shouldn't feel that way.

We quickly learned that to win approval from the adult world it was important to mask what we really felt. Reflexively, we then learned that the best way to accomplish this was to pretend we did not feel. Prodded by insidious little approbations such as, "That's my little man!" or "That's my girl," we learned early on to twist ourselves into the shapes grown-ups expected and approved. No troublesome feelings. No fuss, no muss. Acceptance.

Obviously, all but the rarest among us grow into adulthood without ever being conscious of this universal fiction. However, in the meantime, we have by accretion built up an emotional barrier so stout that now all but the most powerful emotions are kept from invading. We may cry at the movies or feel sad about other people's misfortune or feel outrage about things going on in Washington or the world. But these feelings are as remote from genuine feelings as they are from a knee jerk or an itch. The residue of our all-important interpersonal feelings is so thoroughly and habitually repressed that the potential for violent release may be great. We may be like a pool of oil far beneath the crust of the earth, where the wildcatter's probe sets off the explosive violence of subterranean gases under incalculable pressure for centuries.

This constant flux of feelings is exactly what prevents us from being petrified and rigid. Acknowledgment of feelings is what keeps us in contact with ourselves — perhaps the only communion possible with our own mystery and complexity. We should not underestimate the potential of our feelings, ranking them as inferior to rational thinking. The very fear of acting upon feelings can cause repression, and that leads to impulsive behavior that is blind and dangerous. With each change of tide we are free to refresh our lives, to see anew, to begin again. These feelings, as transient as they may be, are really great opportunities to adjust our being to meet the present moment openly, authentically. We do not have to act upon all of our feelings; however, when we *do* act upon them, we take the helm of our own ship, and with it all the risk of the open seas. Robert Frost said, "I took the path less traveled by, and that has made all the difference."

During the process of growing up, society reinforces all those anti-feeling injunctions: "For God's sake, don't cry." "Oh, you're too sensitive." "Why are you so angry?" This last is often less a question than a statement that, unmasked, would read, "I don't want you to be angry, so if I ask you to explain why you are, I'll divert you to a rational level at which I can make your feelings go away."

Not all therapists deny the existence of feelings, but many encourage *appropriate* feelings and analyze or justify *inappropriate* ones. The criteria for drawing this distinction are neither clear nor compelling.

Consider anger, for example. Anger is an appropriate feeling inasmuch as it is there, having a natural existence inside us; and whatever is natural has to be appropriate. Right? But looked at another way, all anger is inappropriate in the sense that it has little or no value as an information-giving or behavior-forming mechanism. So you see, the appropriate/inappropriate distinction does not work very well. Moreover, it lends itself too readily to a conformity model of human conduct in which *right* feelings are approved and *wrong* ones not endorsed. Having said that, we should concede that while all our natural feelings must be judged appropriate, how we express them may or may not be appropriate.

In expressing our feelings, especially the negative ones, it is important to consider the expression of the other person, the recipient. Your friend, your spouse, or one of your associates hurts your feelings. You feel hurt and angry and want to make your anger known. *How* you verbalize your anger is the issue. Is it revenge, retaliation, getting even that you want? It is good for you to be clear about your intentions. Conceivably, you could ventilate your feelings and feel better, without destroying a relationship. Simply, in specifying the event, you can say, "I was disappointed that you did not call me and tell me you could not meet me for dinner." Think how damaging it could be if you said, "What's wrong with you? Can't you spare a dime to give me a call? You wasted my night. I'll never ask you out to dinner again." The sensitivity of *how* we express feelings is significant.

In short, all feelings are real, all feelings are genuine, all feelings are authentic — simply because they exist. However, they cannot be the sole motivation for action. What you feel does exist. Not far removed from the famous declaration of the French philosopher Descartes — "Cogito, ergo sum," I think, therefore I am — is the expression, "I feel, therefore I am."

So we proceed to some critical observations about *not* being in touch with that reality which your feelings constitute.

1. Although you are not in touch with your feelings, they nevertheless have the strength to program you. What you do not know, or elect not to know, *can* hurt you. It forces you to function artificially and mechanically. In other words, when, through exertion of your willpower or positive thinking, you think you can eliminate feelings, you are deluding yourself. Feelings cannot be eliminated; they can be monitored and controlled, or they can be repressed. They will seek deep subterranean pockets to hide in, only to emerge stealthily in ways you find difficult to identify and understand and control, and in ways others find hard to cope with. Repressed anger, for instance, may surface as sarcasm or ridicule or a hypercritical attitude, all turned against others; or perhaps it may turn against you and appear as migraine headaches or ulcers.

2. At the other end of the spectrum, being out of touch with your feelings produces no such dramatic consequences. On the contrary, life becomes depressingly undramatic, a drag. Without your being able to explain why or perhaps even being actively aware of it, life seems only an ongoing obligation, something to be got through, a Sisyphean responsibility to be discharged unendingly. Remember Sisyphus? He was condemned in Hades to roll a huge boulder up a hill, only to have it constantly roll back down. Usually people awaken to the realization of how drab their life is only when they begin to be in touch with their feelings. In horrified amazement they look back and say, My God, I was bored and depressed all those years and was too anesthetized to realize it! What an incredible waste of myself! How often we hear that poignant refrain.

3. When you are out of touch with your feelings, decisions

are very difficult to make. You cannot determine a should from a wish. You are not sure of what you genuinely want and often find yourself doing things you did not really desire to do.

4. When you are out of touch with your feelings, others find it easy to manipulate you. Ungrounded and uncentered, you live in an other-directed world, a drone locked on to the signals emitted by others — spouse, friends, charismatic gurus, all kinds of experts and authorities — to guide you. You can become so habituated to deferring to others that you no longer have ideas, desires, or hopes of your own.

5. Finally, if you are out of touch with your feelings, it is difficult — all but impossible — to be truly close to other people. Physical contact often becomes a substitute for emotional closeness, which in reality constitutes an effort to avoid such closeness. We have debased the word "intimacy" so that when we hear it, we invariably think of sexual intimacy. Genuine intimacy can be achieved only through the expression of here-and-now feelings, whether positive or negative; otherwise it is pseudo-intimacy.

Encounter groups and most other therapeutic groups provide at least one benefit in that they unblock feelings. Under a skilled leader or with active participants, this exercise can be highly revealing and beneficial. In even the most ineptly handled group, some feelings will surface that you can work with.

Another curious thing about feelings is that we can have feelings about feelings. I can feel guilty about my anger, or embarrassed for having expressed it, or uncomfortable about the way I expressed it. Or I might be afraid of that anger. I might be angrier about those guilt feelings that block me from expressing my original anger. Our feelings can become extraordinarily complicated.

What we invariably find when we start with some seemingly innocuous superficial feeling is that it leads to another feeling just below, and then still to others deeper down, like the stratification of the earth's crust over geological time. Once exposed, that layer makes it possible to explore the layer immediately beneath it. Unlike physical growth, which involves building up the cellular structure, emotional growth requires that we strip away what has been built up, layer by layer, until we reach the primal feelings, such as deep pain and rage. At this bedrock level, the key blocks are broken up and our emotional energy is liberated.

To carry this useful metaphor a little further, articulating our feelings, getting to understand how they relate to each other, is to explore our inner world and come to know ourselves better. Geologists accomplish two important things: by discovering how the terrain was slowly formed, they better understand its characteristics and its behavior; and by studying it closely, they are able to assay the riches it conceals. Therefore, expressing our feelings is beneficial not only for the sense of release it brings, but for the marvelous process of discovery it can set in motion.

One common barrier that blocks contact with our feelings is the notion that every feeling has to be acted on, which is by no means comparable to expressing it. If I am angry with someone, do I have to lash out at that person, or as often as not, at the nearest handy victim? If so, what is my personal gain? Temporary relief? If I have feelings of sexual desire toward someone other than my partner, is it proper to carry them out in action? If I feel frightened, must I avoid the thing I am afraid of? Because this *acting out* usually carries some risk and some cost, we tend to find it convenient to be in charge, that is, to acknowledge the feeling.

If you tend to act on your feelings automatically, you are not in control; they are programming you, your behavior is mechanical, and such behavior is the enemy of freedom and self-identity. To break free of reflexive action requires reflective action. Feelings need to be checked out with the reality principle. Our world beneath the surface is a compressed mass, the layers of our emotional development all fused together. By exploring that subsurface self, we come to know, as does the skilled seismologist, where the fault lines are, where the potential lies for seismic disturbances. Fortunately, this is a world we can control, in greater and greater personal freedom and emotional mastery.

The expression of feeling, essential as it is to interpersonal transactions, is not an end in itself. Although we are often unsure about verbalizing feelings, we are continually articulating our feelings about situations and things, about ourselves and others through nonverbal behavior.

Our feelings find expression even when we would prefer to keep them hidden. Already you may have a whole catalog of feelings about yourself. No doubt you also have developed a wide range of feelings about those closest to you: your spouse, other members of your family, and your friends and associates. Are you comfortable in manifesting them, or are you inclined to fear such openness? Are you willing to articulate your feelings responsibly, both within the close circle of your family, friends, peers, and the broader radius of your day-to-day interpersonal contacts?

Part of your humanity is to have feelings and emotions. If you do not acknowledge and appreciate their legitimacy, they will seem inappropriate to you. You will find feelings to be obstacles to normal interchange with other human beings, rather than commonly shared elements that add color, range, and intensity to interpersonal living. As with most other aspects of behavior, your present style of emotional expression is a *learned* style. Your goal here is more than likely a dual one: to learn modes of expression that will smooth your relations and enhance your interaction with others; and to learn to modulate and temper emotional expressions that are excessive, both for you and for others.

Your feelings should tell exactly who you are in the here-and-now. You should neither manufacture them for proper effect nor mask or repress them because they may seem improper. Your true feelings are an integral part of your humanity, part of the reality that is you.

Some people have trouble expressing even positive feelings. They can cry, grieve, commiserate; they can show how they feel when abused, hurt, rejected; when they are down in the dumps, others know it readily. But they cannot manifest joy, affection, elation, gratitude, peace, contentment, and the like. Others, by contrast, find it easy to give expression to these positive emotions but have not learned to articulate negative ones. Obviously, cultural norms play a large part in whether we learn to reveal or conceal our emotions.

Emotions, in themselves, whether positive or negative, are neither good nor bad. For instance, being angry is not evil; it is simply being human. When negative feelings are expressed destructively, that raises an entirely different question. While it is normal to feel anger, if I express my anger by striking out and injuring another, or by holding it in only to vent it partially in snide remarks and obstructive behavior, then my mode of expressing anger is not constructive. Yet many of us grow up learning that anger, in itself, as with most other negative emotions, is wrong and therefore to be avoided at all costs.

Freedom to express feelings is not license. Emotions can easily be forged into weapons: "I'll dump my anger on him, and it'll serve him right"; or as devices of manipulation: "If I cry, they'll feel guilty and leave me alone." On the other hand, both positive and negative feelings can find constructive expression. You might, for example, say to your spouse or friend, "I'm feeling pretty insecure right now. I've opened up with you about one of my most cherished ambitions in life, and I don't think you've given me much response or support."

This is an honest effort on your part to state your position exactly and to invite the other person to assess a possibly destructive situation.

Here a mildly negative emotion is constructively expressed. Compare it with the following emotional declaration: "Hell, this is the last time I'll ever talk to you about anything. There's not the slightest support. I can spill my guts in front of you, and you just sit there staring at me. Your indifference makes me sick." In this instance, emotions are dumped on your companion. Such dumping, however authentic or justified it may seem, is rarely constructive.

Feelings do not *keep* very well; they should be dealt with as they arise. They should not be saved up and then unloaded on others when they can no longer be contained. Express them when you feel them, in a constructive way, even though they may be negative ones. It is far easier for others to respond to a gradual increase in the intensity of your feelings than to cope with the cumulative final outburst all at once.

What is even worse is our inclination to collect negative emotions, saving them up like trading stamps and then redeeming them all at once by handing them over to the other person, who is unprepared and stunned. It is definitely healthier to deal with both positive and negative feelings as they arise. This vital principle demands that we be ready to explore negative experiences as we encounter them in daily life.

Monitoring or controlling emotions is not at all the same as repressing them. Feelings we try to ignore surface, probably in disguised and distorted ways, despite our efforts to repress them. Bottled-up anger, for instance, leaks out in the form of withheld cooperation, silence, coldness, cynicism, thinly veiled irony. Such forms of emotional expression are obviously destructive, because the other person either responds in kind or does not know how to respond. Emotional control may be said to have a negative side, although only in the same sense that a valve is necessary to impede the flow of a volatile element. It involves keeping the emotions capped and channeled so that they can be directed to achieve communication rather than punishment. Proper control is essentially positive. It does not mean avoiding strong emotions or stifling strong expression of strong emotions. Emotional expression can be both vigorous and disciplined. The following is an example:

> I'm very angry at what you just said. I can see you're not listening to me. I really feel like blowing my stack; something in me wants to punish you. But that wouldn't get either of us anywhere. I want to stay with this and face these issues that are setting us against each other. Now let me repeat slowly what my position is in this matter.

The need for emotional ventilation can be coupled with the desire to work through the issues that give rise to the emotion.

The positive aspect of emotional control might most aptly be labeled *emotional assertiveness*. In situations charged with intense feelings we generally respond in one of three ways: compliantly (nonassertively), aggressively (by attacking), or assertively. Let's consider an example:

> A husband alternates between long periods of withdrawn silence and short spurts of activity and intense interest, at which times he places unusual demands on his wife, expecting her to be as interested and involved as he is — and on his terms. Highly charged and feeling that his partner is indifferent to the whole involvement, he challenges her to respond at his own level of enthusiasm.

His wife's response may fall into one of the following categories:

1. *Nonassertive response.* The wife apologizes for not living up to her husband's expectations. She listens to what he has to say but has little to say in reply. Inwardly, however, she is seething, but she has learned to cap a display of her emotions. Later, she

tells a friend how furious she is with her husband. The relief is momentary. She still feels empty and impotent.

2. *Aggressive response.* As the wife listens to what the husband has to say, her temperature climbs rapidly, and then she lashes out at him angrily. She accuses him of being two-faced, of not practicing what he preaches. There is no real interchange; it could be described as a diatribe. Not only are the immediate feelings being dumped, but a heavy load of pent-up resentments is poured forth. Then she feels temporary relief; she has exhausted herself, and the storm subsides. Soon comes the feeling of guilt, of defeat; because she has burned her bridges, the sense of isolation is more acute, and the husband is participating in her punishment.

3. *Assertive response.* She listens to what he has to say, indicates briefly that she understands the issue, and thinks it may be valid, but she would like time to think about it alone; she arranges an appropriate time later when she will discuss it with him. She takes the opportunity to let him know that even though he may have had reason to challenge her, other feelings she has make it difficult for her to respond to that challenge as constructively as she would like to. Her contribution to the ensuing dialogue might run along these lines:

> In all honesty, I find myself resenting your challenge, not because it doesn't have merit, for it does, but because it fails to take into account the erratic way we interact as partners. My experience is that you're really totally present only at times, usually in short unpredictable spurts. Then, for long spells you're withdrawn and uncommunicative. I've mentioned this before, and I've confessed it bothers me. I want more than anything to share your interests, but it isn't easy when the door is so seldom open. I would like us to be more open to one another; that's why I've spoken my feelings this way.

Assertive response allows for emotional ventilation at its most refreshing, and it does not slam any doors. More often than not, it opens new ones to fuller communication and more rewarding partnership.

Thoughts to Ponder

- Most people are ruled by their feelings and think nothing strange about the fact that they have so little to say about their own lives. Could you make decisions or design your life by merely obeying your feelings?

- When you are charged with emotions, positive (such as loving) or negative (such as being angry), can you make a serious decision such as to get married or relocate or change your job? For better or worse, many people who are emotionally charged make serious decisions.

- Feelings/emotions are not reasons; they are only the steam we generate to drive us toward our objectives. Granted, we could pursue our objectives without steam, but feelings and emotions make us go faster. Thoughts are mainly conditioned by limited experience. Feelings originate in the authentic self.

- Many individuals use their likes or dislikes as a compass to find which way the emotional wind is blowing. Likes and dislikes are merely conditioned responses we *learned in childhood* and have no significance; they have become habits. Could you really live your life by focusing only on what pleases you?

- Feelings/emotions are triggered by our thought processes. Think of something good and you get a good feeling. Think of something bad and the result is a negative feeling. If we modify our thoughts, our feelings will be different.

- Most of us guard and protect our likes and dislikes as if they were more precious than life itself; some people have died in an effort to protect and indulge their appetites. Emotions die on the vine if we do not water them with our tears.

- We have no record that feelings and emotions ever solved a problem. On the contrary, we have multiple documents reporting that action and movement have solved most serious problems. Emotions tend to slow down the activity; therefore, the problem is prolonged. In order to maintain a sort of initiative, we may have to be in charge of our emotions.

Chapter 14

What Do Men Want?

The battle of the sexes stems from the blindness
of men and women to each other's uniqueness.

—Herbert Holt

In all stages of human development, we find the male gender
dissatisfied. Something is not quite right. Changes in a man's relationship to himself and to the external world are taking place,
and each change causes both discomfort and dissatisfaction.

The boy's world gradually expands. Leaving the family and
entering the world sometime after the age of sixteen, the young
man has to make many adjustments. He must separate himself
from the security of his home and connect with the insecurity
of society. He must form a sense of *reality* that allows him to accept his surroundings as having an independent existence not
necessarily subject to his control. If he comes from a dysfunctional family, and most of us do, adjustment to an adult world
becomes more complex.

As the male forms a stronger sense of who he is and what
he wants and gains a more realistic view of the world — what it
is like, what it offers him and demands from him — disappointment sets in. The world is not as he perceived it, and it demands
a lot from him. However, as he grows older and senses himself
to be separate from the world, he becomes more self-generating
and independent. In the process, he gains confidence and makes
more connections with the world. As a result, he feels more
fully part of it.

In early adult transition, a boy-man begins his novitiate in the adult world and takes an important step of exploration and initial choice toward establishing an occupation and fashioning a life structure. Depending in large part upon how well he adjusts at this time, he forms a valued adult identity and becomes capable of living with a greater degree of autonomy. He has more responsibility for himself and others and gains competence in his various social roles.

Settling down ordinarily occupies the span between the early and late thirties. During this period, a man makes deeper commitments, invests more of himself in his work, family, and valued interests, and pursues long-range plans and goals. He establishes his niche in society, digs in, builds a base, and goes after what he wants, within a defined pattern. In an effort to "make it," he plans, strives, moves onward and upward, following an inner timetable that specifies minor goals and the stages that he aspires to reach. He hopes that by a certain age he will be earning a stated income and that by a certain age he will be on a stated rung on his way up the ladder of success.

In the mid- to late thirties, he begins to feel an inner strength: "I have to become my own man." He has felt overly dependent upon and constrained by persons and groups who have authority over him or who exert great influence on him. Impatiently, he awaits the time when he will have the authority to make his own decisions. The sense of constraint may occur not only in work but also in marriage. Support from parents or parental figures and advice from friends or mentors are limited at best, nonexistent at worst. In these years, a man struggles toward a crucial promotion or advancement in status or some significant recognition such as being known as a first-rate person in his chosen field. In his yearning to be validated by some external power — colleagues, family members, society — he seems to be living in a state of suspended animation.

In the meantime, *middle-life transition* occurs, whether he succeeds or fails in his search for affirmation by society. The central issue is not whether he succeeds or fails in his goals. Rather, the issue is what to do with the *experience of disparity* between what he has gained and what he wants for himself. The sense of disparity between "What have I reached at this point?" and "What do I really want?" instigates a disturbing dissatisfaction.

If a dissatisfied man does not succumb to chronic depression, he may have some healthy reactions. In an introspective self-inventory during this period, a man may ask himself, What do I have to show for my life? Do I want to go on doing what I have been doing for the years I have left? What doors are open to me at my age?

Often the response leads to positive payoffs in his career, personality, and family life. He can experience an invigorating rebirth, generating new energies and new commitments. He comes out of the transitional stage of life reorganized around new objectives and satisfactions. Most men at this age have developed certain skills, and they start thinking about reclaiming dormant interests in other fields. This accounts for *second careers* — a mechanic opens his own shop, a top executive deserts the rat-race and teaches in a community college. Wendell S., president of an educational video company, came through this soul-searching period with such a powerful sense of being his *own man* that he resigned to become an independent consultant. He moved to Sandpoint, Idaho, found a most desirable location by a lake, and established a residence. As he relaxed and explored the area, he decided to enter the real estate business. After a few purchases and sales, Wendell realized that he had found what he wanted. He began to write poetry, developed an art gallery, and established Swan's Landing Restaurant. Now he is more satisfied with himself than he ever was.

Ideally, men could prepare themselves for the vicissitudes of the frenzied forties and fifties. It definitely helps to follow sensible health practices in diet and exercise to reach middle age in good physical shape. Maintaining close friendships and understanding family relationships are also important for psychological balance.

A man who has been self-reliant and a rational problem solver in his twenties and thirties tends to do better as he grows chronologically older. Then, even if he becomes physically ill, he can regard himself as unimpaired, compared to the passive, nonassertive type who is apt to whine and complain.

Stanley, a thirty-nine-year-old mechanic, sank into a chair in my office and sighed. He looked dazed and miserable, and tears filled his eyes. "I want to save my marriage. I love my wife." Unable to ventilate his feelings, he sobbed.

"What seems to be the problem?" I asked.

"I had an affair and told my wife about it."

"What is it that you want from me?"

"To help me save my marriage."

"Do you love your wife?"

"Very much." Tears trickled down his face.

"I think I can help you," I said and proceeded to get information about Stanley. In another year he would be forty. He sensed failure in his job, failure at home where his wife lacked understanding of his needs, failure in society. Nonetheless, he assured me that he wanted to save his marriage, for he truly loved his wife. I believed him.

That same day, he went home, packed his suitcases, and moved out of his house to an unknown address. A year later, his wife, still in shock, wondered, "How could he do such a thing?" She showed me cards and letters that he had sent her during the three months prior to his sudden departure; they were written with unprecedented sensitivity and love. She displayed the extravagant and expensive jewelry he had given her for their fifteenth anniversary.

Apart from the feelings of mental fatigue, physical exhaustion, and marital discontent that propelled Stanley out of the household, I believe that he was unconscious of the major reason for his separation from his wife. He was in search of the idealized mother, who in real life does not exist. His domineering mother turned him into a passive man devoted to pleasing women in the hope that one of them might adore him. Once married, he continued to expect that his wife would adore him if only he were well-behaved. When the early romantic years were succeeded by reality, his search for adoration caused him to leave his marriage. Stanley was basically a dissatisfied man. A large majority of men, young and old, are going through their lives with a neurotic or self-defeating attitude. Some of them are of the opinion that their condition is *not their fault*.

Truly, it is easier to blame dissatisfaction with one's job or one's spouse on circumstances than to come to grips with reality, that is, with minimum anxiety to accept things that cannot change and to make a concerted effort to *change* whatever is realistically changeable to meet your needs today.

Like Stanley and other dissatisfied males, we are daily confronted with a critical question: What can I do to live a happier, more productive, and more peaceful life? People have been looking for an answer to this question since the beginning of history. The answer is not to be found in the fates or horoscopes or in philosophical theories or even in therapeutic encounters, but in ourselves, in our own consciousness.

Not too long ago one of my clients died of a massive heart attack. He was fifty-four, and several members of his family said hard work killed him. As his therapist, I think that what he really died of was knowing he would never have the courage to live. Joey, the name he wished to be known by, was the good son and husband and father who worked very hard and reached the top of the ladder of success, becoming the top executive of his company. During his years of service, he gained promotion after promotion, became more successful than he probably ever wanted to be, and earned a six-digit salary. Joey was an unhappy man. In an outburst of frustration, he blurted out, "I would be happier if I owned a bicycle shop." I believed him. His voice was angry. He worked six days a week and many evenings to meet the needs of the company and maintain the admiration of those around him. Eventually, he was too tired and busy to talk to his wife and children.

There are thousands of such men, who lead short and un-lived lives of meeting other people's expectations, of obeying other people's perceptions of who and what they are. We judge and pronounce a sentence against a man who kills another man. What action do we take against a man who kills himself gradually through living a tense, anxious, and meaningless life in which there is hardly a sense of exultation or joy in being the man he might have been?

It may well be that men are paid higher salaries than women and are not discriminated against by colleagues and employers, as women too often are, but their lives are often more oppressed than those of women. Women tend to be more aware of themselves and their problems. They are able to verbalize their feelings without hesitation. Their emotional apparatus is often far more advanced than that of men. *Women feel freely.* They feel their angers and their loves; they feel their frustrations and fears; and they are constantly examining and reassessing their lives. Thus, they are less likely to develop ulcers and heart ailments, which are common in men. Men are less flexible, less defensive, have less insight, and find it less threatening to deny their feelings. Although they do not openly complain, they are, generally speaking, dissatisfied with their lives.

As they approach the middle years, men seem to be far

more unhappy than women and are much less in touch with their feelings. They tend to act out whatever they feel. They go through a teenage resurgence; they buy a red sports convertible, dress chic, act "cool," and reach out for new experiences; they test their sexuality with a younger woman, and they divorce their wives and leave their families. *They change.* Do they? I find them more oppressed than women — and not by anyone but themselves. Of course, their dissatisfaction is caused by a complicated web of factors: the culture we grow up in teaches men not to cry, to be brave, to be totally responsible for the security of wives and children, and not to express their loving feelings too openly.

In an affluent society, most men in pursuit of the American dream still believe that enthusiasm for sports, owning expensive homes, going on luxurious vacations, and making a handsome salary are the measure of a real man.

Anyone who accepts this notion of what constitutes a *real man* inevitably gets into the habit of competing with others, as if competition were a law of nature. This is a costly misunderstanding, since human skills develop adequately only in cooperation, a condition of reinforcement. Competition grows out of dependence. It imitates initiative in a deceptive way and thus clouds our understanding. The competitive individual trains himself to outrun his pacemaker, and we may imagine that he is enjoying the fruits of initiative. He often develops much skill so that he appears masterful and competent. As a result of his success, he is often put in a key position where he must originate and organize policy in an unstructured situation that demands independent, imaginative, original planning. In such a situation, he cannot function inventively, since he has trained himself only to outrun or imitate *existing patterns*; he has no freedom of mind to create or improvise new forms. He spends his working days joyless, unfulfilled, in a bind or trap.

He may not suffer from debilitating fixations or nervous ailments, but he complains of vague, diffuse dissatisfactions with life and feels his amorphous existence to be futile and purposeless. Recently, a businessman described his condition: he has a subtly experienced yet pervasive feeling of emptiness, violent oscillations of self-esteem and a general inability to get along. He gains a sense of heightened self-esteem only by attaching himself to strong, admired figures whose acceptance he craves and by whom he needs to feel supported. Although he carries out his daily responsibilities and even achieves distinction, happiness eludes him, and life frequently strikes him as not worth living.

Developmentally, most men are taught to be tender to women and children, under certain circumstances, but never to show such feelings toward other men. How sad! Last summer, my friend Theodore and I were walking along University Street in Athens, Greece. Simultaneously, we placed our arms around each other's waist and enjoyed the afternoon stroll talking about common interests. At one moment, I turned to my wife, who was walking beside me, and said, "Pat, can you visualize Theodore and me walking in such an intimate way somewhere in the United States?"

"No way. I'd have a hard time accepting that," she replied.
"Why?"

"Because such intimacy is not in our American tradition."

Over the years, as I deal with male dissatisfactions, including my own, I feel the pain of men's loneliness, the weakening of male relationships, and gradual disillusionment with male friends. It is strange that men may have wives whom they love and cherish, they may even have women friends, but their relationships with other men, which could be a reflection of their own manhood, are generally on the surface, insincere, and at times hypocritical. There is a great deal of confusion between the words "friend" and "acquaintance." When we think of every acquaintance as a friend, we can get into trouble. We have high expectations of our friends, and, parallel with that, we have a responsibility toward them.

Men who do not let themselves think or feel about the real meaning of friendship usually conceal or slough off their disappointment. Others feel guilty for not doing justice to their male friends, or they lower their expectations. An honest look around us provides convincing evidence that there is an essential friendlessness among men. There is some justification for the lyrics of the Greek song "Friends No Longer Exist":

> Friends no longer exist
> Who love with extra caring.
> The one who claims he does,
> He loves for his own interest.

You may remember the time when you were younger, you believed in true friendship, you thought you were prepared to die to save a friend's life, you were convinced true friendship was yours, and you had, perhaps as late as army or college life, at least one man with whom you were deeply connected. Doesn't this memory bring back a glowing smile? Where is that friend now?

When I visit my childhood friends in the little village in Greece where I grew up, they ask me what I do for a living. I tell them that I practice psychotherapy. "Oh, here we don't need psychotherapy; we have friends," they reply.

"What happens when you have problems?"

"We sit in the coffee-shop and discuss them with friends."

That is a sort of group therapy, I suppose, and it's their way.

"Normal" men and women, completely satisfied people, are hard to find. In our own peculiar ways, we try with more or less success to wrestle with the fundamental, insoluble problems and contradictions of life, such as the longing to enjoy childish dependency on the one hand and independent existence on the other; the desire to connect with other people and the fear of them and of our own aggression; the fear of death and the aspiration to live forever through fame and fortune; the wish for power and control over others and the wish of subordination; love and hate; humility and hubris — the list appears never ending. In this regard, everyone is more or less dissatisfied. However, our psychological abilities to come to terms with the strength of our inner self, being various and diverse, are our only hope. In spite of our peculiarities and distortions, we make significant strides by confronting our resistance to change.

You men are living at an important and critical moment now, for it is clear to you that the images of adult manhood given to you by society and popular culture are worn out; you can no longer depend upon them. You know that by the time you are thirty-five, the images of the "right man," the "true man" that you acquired in high school do not work in real life.

Like patterns in a kaleidoscope, man changes dramatically as each decade turns. Forty years ago the American male appeared with some consistency that became the model of manhood. He supported his family with responsible labor, admired discipline, ignored women's emotional needs, and appreciated his own body. Unless he had an enemy to fight, he remained emotionally passive. The 1950s male was supposed to stand up for the United States, never cry, and always provide.

Another sort of man appeared in the 1960s. The conflict in Vietnam raised many doubts about the male image. If manhood implied going to a foreign country to fight, did any sensible adult want any part of it? To what purpose?

Another image emerged in the 1970s. The image became that of a soft, tender, attentive male who appreciated life, did not want war, and was concerned about damage to the earth. He had a gentle attitude toward women and was supportive of their equal rights cause. He had little energy to offer, however, and action was not for him.

In the 1980s, there was a marked change in the image, and greed became the outstanding attribute. Emphasis was placed on salary increases, real estate transactions boomed, and material prosperity was the measure of the great man and the good life. The American dream was coming to fruition, and, as the calendar moved into the 1990s, the dream became a nightmare. The recession made its unwelcome appearance, and men found themselves jobless and in debt, cheated out of their ambition to be all that they could be.

The nation's spirits revived for a short period during the Persian Gulf War when national unity and pride took center stage. Peacetime conditions returned, and men found themselves as they were before the war, jobless and in debt, listening to political promises of a recovery in the national economy.

In view of our changing image, briefly exemplified above, we men need to diffuse our anguish by realizing that the images of adult manhood given by turning time will continue to change. We cannot rely on them for our emotional sustenance. The image formulated in one decade is replaced by another in the succeeding decade, leaving men with the agonizing question, Who am I? or What should I be? The grief in men has been increasing steadily since the Industrial Revolution, and the grief has reached a depth that cannot be ignored.

The dissatisfaction is clear. Silently and restlessly, men exploit the earth's resources, devalue and humiliate women, and fight for power. Upper hierarchies work hard to keep men as boys and entangle both men and women in systems of industrial domination.

Greed and materialistic superiority propel governments to

engage in long-term preparation for war. Men look for or we invent enemies against whom we must be ready to fight. The most startling thing about our history is that we have always been at war with one another. We can measure our advancement in the sophistication of devices we have created over the decades for the purpose of killing off our brothers. Our arsenals have evolved from simple weapons of destruction to automatic machines that can kill multitudes in a few seconds. We pride ourselves on having the most catastrophic weaponry to conquer and defeat the enemy. Our emphasis on enemies rather than on allies has brought us again and again to the brink of destruction. It is a strange phenomenon that the greatest minds of our time, who thus far have dedicated themselves to the discovery of the most destructive weapons, do not engage themselves in the miracle of life and work out plans and means for peaceful co-existence and harmony among nations. Is it a naive notion to think of peace and harmony? Perhaps. One of the best ways for men to begin to put this naive notion to work is to pay attention to how we function in relation to our immediate environment, relatives, friends, and co-workers.

Regardless of the current images about men's personal life and living, we are still the artist, director, and producer of our *new life*. Our circumstances up to this point will not determine what our life will be. Once we visualize the image that we want, the appropriate emotion and consequent behavior will flow automatically. We must understand that the opportunity for realizing the desired image is up to each one of us and that the physical reality is already here, on this planet and available for us to make the connection. Our job as visualizer is to learn to bring it from the world of thought to the physical world of form. In order to make a visualization a reality in the world of form, we must be willing to do whatever it takes to make it happen. The Greek philosopher Diogenes held a lantern and searched for an honest man during the daylight, but we need to hold our lantern close and look for the *real man* within ourselves. This task becomes less cumbersome as we look for the "universal man," *homo sapiens*, emulating past and present exemplary lives that may enrich our own efforts. This is the single most important aspect of visualization and imagery. Everything that we can picture in our minds is already here waiting for us to connect to it. What needs to be added is our state of willingness. If we men want to make our new image a reality in our lives, we must be willing to do what we have to do and remind ourselves that we cannot fail if we try to be ourselves. We can only produce results.

Thoughts to Ponder

- Our approach to life as men is the result of early programming and self-training. We can change our condition later in life when we realize that our disturbing responses — nonproductivity, negativity, passivity, lack of motivation — are nothing more than inappropriate, inadequate holdovers from childhood.

- As adults we are expected to replace boyhood behavior with more useful responses so that we may be a help rather than a burden to our environment. It is useless for us to try to escape the pain we create for ourselves as we seek to solve adult problems with the tricks and evasions of a boy.

- The problems of behavior that make us feel and act like inferior, third-class passengers in life are no more than the fruits of our failure to develop the habit of both emotional and physical self-reliance. Many of us maintain the mistaken notion — carried from our boyhood — that others should take care of us emotionally and physically and that others should be deeply interested in us and be responsible for our welfare. Such a notion may be a covert need that ostensibly is denied.

- Dependency is the root of all feelings of inferiority. The leaning on others emotionally or physically is a child's way of life. It generates the third-class citizenship mentality. Out of this grows the habit of envy, making us focus on the success of others, ignoring our own potential, and viewing the world with a negative eye.

- Unhappiness, loneliness, neurotic symptoms, crime, and similar distresses originate from the unresolved habit of leaning and depending on others. As we lean on others, they control, dominate, and exploit us for their own benefit.

- When we accept our own strengths and weaknesses, synthesize our positive and negative qualities, and become self-reliant emotionally and physically, we can function as mature adult human beings. Then we can cooperate with other adults, recognizing that life demands that we be productive and useful.

- The inadequate responses of envy, greed, competition, and sabotage, with which men try to solve the problems of life, are reactions that would not arise in the first place if we were in the habit of standing on our own two feet.

- Our problems do not have mysterious, hidden sources, and we do not have to look far or deep to find their origin; we stumble, trip, and fall over the origin all day long, refusing to identify it as our own naive childish attitude.

- All human beings are subjected to changes; men share the inheritance of all human potentialities and are equally based in evolution and growth. All human beings can evoke their store of potentialities, shape them into their own creation, and discover their own reality. We are our own architects, and we design life to meet our needs and wishes. Whatever one human being has done in life can be done by others. Creativity is a built-in attribute in each of us. It waits, however, for the awakening touch of individual initiative to activate its parts and shape its aspects.

Chapter 15

What Do Women Want?

Except for the child, woman's creation is so often invisible. A woman does not see the results of her giving as concretely as man does in his work.

—*Anne M. Lindbergh*

The differences between men and women are clearly seen in the family and in society, and we must make an effort to eliminate their unfair and harmful crystallization of rigid stereotypes and prejudices.

We know that masculine and feminine principles exist. All people, both male and female, experience both masculinity and femininity in themselves, although in unique forms and different proportions.

Each person is a unique combination of these energies. When we look at women on the whole, we find that they are more attuned to the feminine principle, have greater access to it, and have a higher percentage of it in their psychological make-up. Similarly, men are more attuned to the masculine principle. Of course this is a generality. Some men are psychologically more feminine than many women, and some women are psychologically more masculine than many men.

Only by accepting both masculine and feminine principles, bringing them together, and harmonizing them within ourselves will we be able to transcend the conditioning of our roles and discover the source of our dissatisfactions.

Beckie dashed into my office like an Olympic runner and flung herself into the soft leather chair that she had occupied every Tuesday morning for her therapy sessions during the past six weeks. "I don't know why I'm here. Nothing seems to change. I still feel empty." She blinked her eyes and sighed. Her anxiety was evident.

"My husband and I are in love," she continued. "He's a fine man. My two daughters — one in college and the other graduating from high school in June — are a delight. My career is blossoming; I got two promotions last year. My church is interesting and inspiring. I do aerobics three times a week, so physically I'm in top shape. But, still, something is missing. I feel a void within." She folded her arms tightly and crossed her legs.

I glanced through the window to get my brain in gear. The sky was blue and the sun bright and warm, an unusual January day for New Jersey. Beckie's freshly polished red Jaguar was parked in my driveway. My mind's eye caught a glimpse of mythology: Andromeda, the beautiful maiden chained to a rock on the shore, waiting to be devoured by the sea monster. I turned quickly to face Beckie. She looked sad. Who, I wondered, could be the god-gifted Perseus who would rescue the victim from her chains and lead her to greener pastures?

Between her frequent sighs and occasional smiles I could sense that something beyond both her awareness and mine was causing her anxiety, and she was seeking therapy in the hope of finding a concrete answer to her dilemma. In the abyss of her psyche an undefined conflict lingered, causing dissatisfaction with what appeared to be, at least externally, a good life.

Dissatisfaction with something in life is a common characteristic among humans. An ancient adage claims: There is no hope for the satisfied. There is always something to make us fret; no matter how much we possess, we want more; we look at our situation and think things should be different. Our souls are troubled until they return to their creator, said St. Augustine. It is my personal observation that women, because of their intricate and incredibly complex emotional apparatus — being honest with their feelings and willing to express them — are more overtly dissatisfied than men. As with the mythical snake-haired Gorgon Medusa, the emotional forces writhe around in their heads — in their psyches — leaving them troubled and occasionally turning their male counterparts into stone.

Most men have trouble dealing with emotions; they prefer to deal with logic and rational thinking. When a woman expresses unfavorable feelings, men feel threatened. Perhaps they are afraid they may not be able to satisfy a woman emotionally or face their part of responsibilities, and this fear causes them to shrink away lest their manhood be challenged.

Men often think of the involvement and the responsibilities of parenthood, but seldom do we admit that women carry the heavier part of the parenting load. Women are the carriers of culture and tradition, passing values from one generation to the next, while the male counterpart has eyes on the future — constantly breaking new ground. This leaves women lagging behind. The values they are trying to preserve with their children are seldom valued in the progressive world modeled by men. There is a gap that separates women from men — figuratively speaking. This becomes more evident during the early stages of motherhood. While the mother is involved with the infant, her husband continues to be involved with the world, hardly participating in the arduous task of mothering. If the woman happens to be employed outside the home, as most women are, she is also expected to take care not only of the infant but of domestic affairs as well. As she invests years in raising the children, the man works to advance his career, perhaps for the sake of his family. One can well understand why women complain that they do not get enough attention or appreciation from men. Can any male fathom the emotional and physical contribution of a woman to her family? It is refreshing to see some men have become aware, and they make themselves available in spite of the existing stereotypes. Kahlil Gibran in his book *The Broken Wings* summarizes men's perceptions:

> The poets and writers are trying to understand the reality of woman, but up to this day they have not understood the hidden secrets of her heart, because they look upon her from behind the sexual veil and see nothing but externals; they look upon her through a magnifying glass of lust and find nothing except weakness and submission.

This is certainly a gloomy picture of how some men see women; we can imagine how women must feel if they are perceived this way.

What are really *the hidden secrets of her heart?* I can only give a male point of view.

A woman wants to:

- give and receive love
- make her man happy
- harmonize the world around her
- build a warm nest, a home
- give birth
- see her children happy
- be creative

She wants and secretly *expects* reciprocity in all whom she gives. She also wants *visibility*, that her efforts be noticed and appreciated. That is the reward she longs for. But above all, a woman wants to be loved not because of what she can give to a man and to life but because of *who* she is as a person.

Anne Morrow Lindbergh enriches the above list with her contribution:

> Woman wants perpetually to spill herself away. All her instinct as a woman — the eternal nourisher of children, of men, of society — demands that she gives. Her time, her energy, her creativeness drain out into these channels if there is any change, any leak. Traditionally we are taught, and instinctively we long, to give where it is needed — and immediately. Eternally, woman spills herself away in driblets to the thirsty, seldom being allowed the time, the quiet, the peace, to let the pitcher fill up to the brim.

If it is a woman's function to give, she must be replenished. How? If women were convinced that *time out,* a day off or an hour of solitude were a reasonable ambition, they would find a way of attaining it. It is more a question of inner convictions than of outer pressures, though of course the outer pressures are there and make scheduling more difficult.

In solitude, women will find the true essence of themselves, the stilling of the soul around the activities of the mind and body. There lies her divine destiny, her *dynamis,* her power. A woman can contribute to society the higher aspects of her femininity — altruistic love, compassion, the sense of and respect for life, qualities with which she is usually more familiar and which she can often express with greater facility than can a man. A woman chooses not to go to war or to prepare for war or to discover destructive weapons. Rather, she will choose to get involved with social and political life for a healthy purpose.

At times, her passion for life is her soul, and sexuality manifests this. A woman abandons herself in passion in the moment that soul and body are one. This can happen with a man that she, in the first place, trusts and, in the second, loves. Trust is first because it is her soul she is abandoning when she gives herself to passion. When a woman makes love — not genital love, but a surrendering of her total being — she becomes a creator and comes to herself as a living soul. The sexual/spiritual energies woven together create not necessarily a physical child but a spiritual one, a relationship. It is within this experience that man and woman come to realize the *mystery* of life.

In my twenty years of practice in psychotherapy, I have found the phenomenon of women's dissatisfaction to be a nagging reality, and in recent consultations four of my colleagues, two men and two women, concurred with my findings.

During the past twelve months, I have dealt consistently with the same ten couples who have come to see me once a week for marital counseling. Each couple invested one hour per week and a considerable amount of money to explore their problems and possibly find a *cure* for them. In nine couples out of the ten, the woman was the dissatisfied partner, the man passively claiming that the marriage or relationship was just fine. Of course a man has a hard time admitting *his* contribution toward the failure of the relationship. He prefers to ignore the problem or deny that there is one. The tenth woman claimed that she wanted to learn some coping skills; the stress she was experiencing in her marriage was overwhelming her.

The state of being chronically dissatisfied can have toxic consequences in any relationship. Think for a moment of the constant complainer who suffers such malaise. Nothing satisfies the complainer, who either alienates or causes bad feelings in those around him or her. In a marital relationship, the consequences of chronic dissatisfaction can be disastrous, causing brutal abuse or divorce or eventual deterioration.

Each couple was an interesting study. Wendy, in her early thirties, married for ten years, was a top-notch homemaker. She loved her husband and he loved her. He was thirty-six, handsome, strong and athletic, an architect. They were always together, and since they had no children, they had time for tennis, dancing, traveling, and enjoying their common interests in plays, concerts, movies, and books. He seemed content with the marriage. Life was almost perfect — but not quite. Something was missing; Wendy was not sure what it was, but she knew she was dissatisfied. She spoke about her life: "So I left home in search of a career. I dressed in executive suits, tailoring myself to the specifications of the world. I stripped my body of flesh, my heart of the overflow of feeling, and my language of exuberant and dramatic imprecisions. I cut back the flight of my fancy, made my thought rigorous, and subjected it to measures of demonstration and proof, trying not to talk with my hands, trying hard to subdue my voice, getting my burst of laughter under control. My male colleagues perceived me as a well-rounded personality, fun to be with, and a confident businessperson, but I felt miserably unhappy within."

I asked Wendy what went wrong, and she said, "I tried so hard to be taken seriously that I made life difficult for myself. I was afraid that men would think me kooky, frivolous. Well, if I have to be on my guard and play a role, I'm not going to be happy at work."

Evelyn had been married for twelve years, and in her quiet, lonely moments, the thought that this was all life had to offer frightened her. In her mid-forties, she could have been a model, and she had a husband who "adores" her. She was obsessed with an insatiable desire to succeed in her profession and had already become one of the vice presidents in an investment firm on Wall Street. It is not difficult to sense the set of weighty problems that her ambition created. She wanted to be considered equal to her male counterparts, but that did not happen. She was equal in title, but not equal in salary, not equal in professional treatment, not equal in socializing. Explanations were given: "He's a man; he needs more money." In major meetings, her contributions were overlooked. Although a rotating system was used, she was never allowed to chair a meeting.

There is nothing unique about Evelyn's experience. Women at all levels, across all professions, do not make as much money as men, which accounts in part for women's dissatisfaction. "I work harder than most men I know; I'm very good at what I do, and I'm committed to my job and company," said Susan, an executive of the finance and budgeting section of another major firm. "My bosses give me glowing evaluations, but they don't put their money where their mouths are. If a man got such evaluations, he'd make twice the salary I do."

Regardless of why women are not earning what they think they deserve, their salaries strongly affect their self-image. The majority claim that, all things considered, they think of themselves as being successful. Most successful seem to be those who earn most money. While in the eyes of the world they appear successful, 70 percent are unhappy with their careers. Apart from their complaint of being underpaid, a key reason for their discontent lies in the degree of authority granted them. Eighty-five percent of women believe that they do not have the authority they need to accomplish their tasks. Susan shook with anger when she spoke about the small amount of clout she exercised. "I have been recently assigned the project of making an ineffectual department of my company profitable within a year. To carry out this task, I need the power to hire and fire whom I choose, to apportion my budget as I see fit, and to make decisions. My bosses don't want to give me that power. Therefore, the fate of the division and my own fate are in jeopardy." Susan's frustration is understandable, and so it is with many women who are entrusted with major responsibilities but not empowered to perform them.

During this writing, Susan suffered another blow from the upper hierarchy. Her job was assigned to a man who was brought in by her boss. She felt deeply hurt, and to quote her own words, "I know my job well, and regardless of where the company places me, I will feel okay. But what hurts most is the injustice done to me because I'm a woman. The man who took my place started with a salary of $101,000, plus $42,000 annual bonus. After ten years of employment in the same company, I was receiving only $60,000 and no bonus. The man who replaced me was given three assistants to do the job that I was doing alone. I'm infuriated."

Many are the injustices in our world, but the discrimination against women is a most painful one. We need to stand firm in our convictions, patient and persistent in our efforts, if we aspire to see some major changes in our society.

The housewife concept is another area that has been taken for granted. While the husband is at work, the all-encompassing domestic job is assigned to the wife at home. A wife who allows her husband to do nothing — "my husband is not used to doing domestic chores" — upholds the theory that housework is a woman's job. In addition, she reinforces dependency needs in her husband. Spouses who desire to maintain a creative relationship realize that housework is part of married life, and they pitch in and do their share without being asked. One takes over where the other leaves off. As tedious as the job may seem, the man who takes some responsibility for housework will experience a great feeling, a sense of belonging.

The other seven couples suffered a sort of domestic dissatisfaction: faulty communication, poor money management, intrusive in-laws, deviant children, unsatisfactory sex — areas that an average marriage therapist clarifies, shows how to ameliorate by developing options, and reconstructs. When spouses are willing to work on the marriage, such therapy is successful. In the case of these women, they were willing to do the necessary work, but they shared a common complaint that they felt they were unable to work on: lack of attention from their husbands.

- He's not as exciting as he used to be.

- He doesn't want to do anything on the weekends.

- He's too passive. He won't help with the chores.

- He's too involved with his work.

- He's emotionally detached from the kids.

- He doesn't fix anything around the house.

- He's not ambitious.

- He's always in front of the television.

A woman might raise a question at this point: "If these present obstacles, should I stop my growth? Should they spoil my happiness?"

Although single women may see the world differently from married ones, psychotherapists' offices are inundated with them as well. Many dissatisfied single women are frustrated, suffer emotional turmoil, and continue to return to painful relationships to recapture their fantasies and to try to heal the ills they suffer. Men and women find fantasies equally sweet as long as they last. However, many women wallow in fantasies; men feed into them, and women usually pay the price of abandonment.

Shirley had survived an unexpected betrayal after a seven-year relationship. A woman of integrity and strong values, she put the pieces together, and life made sense again. At this point, Mr. Charming appeared on the horizon, and things began to expand beyond her expectations. In the third week of their meeting, Mr. Charming inundated Shirley's life with luscious lunches, expensive dinners, and presents. She felt overwhelmed. Being straightforward, she asked him what it all meant. He replied, "You're the woman of my dreams." Who would not be charmed by such a compliment? Shirley visualized a future with this man. She thought of him as God's gift. She wanted to marry him. He constituted most of the things her heart desired; he was handsome, had a good job, and was generous, loving, and sociable. When she introduced the idea of a home, he took her to an exclusive neighborhood and asked her to choose the style of house she would really like to spend her life in. That night, Mr. Charming arrived at Shirley's apartment with another man whom he introduced as the architect who was to design their dream house. However, since he was going overseas for two weeks, the plans would be delayed. He was hoping to return with samples of European styles, confirming that he preferred the unusual. The night ended in excitement and joviality — and in the disappearance of Mr. Charming. Although shocked at first, Shirley came to realize she had been taken for a fantasy trip by a first-class faker. She felt angry with herself for being so easily taken in, but how could she have known?

Who becomes frustrated? The woman, of course. At times a woman falls in love with a man who is not real; she falls in love with her fantasies. The man brings her into his world of fantasy: "Where have you been all my life? You are the woman of my dreams!" Nothing seems impossible. They both love the dream world. Suddenly one of them wakes up and says, "I have to choose the real world." We need to get up every morning and face the responsibilities of life, work, respect for the rights of others, and willingness to give part of self for the sustenance of society.

Marianne had never been married. With parted lips and limpid eyes, heartbroken, she sat facing me. She was her father's walking doll, a sacrificing friend eager to meet the needs of her periodic mates and at the same time, a demanding woman. Her willing submission to her lovers resulted in broken relationships, overly critical attitudes, drivenness, migraines, and other symptoms of tension that Marianne sought to release at the spa, the shopping mall, and the beauty salon. The love that she was willing to make available to the other was no longer available to her. She felt drained and was physically and emotionally fragile. As long as she could fantasize her love, she identified with the positive side of her father-god, for love in her fantasies was the idealized innocent love a daughter has for her father. Once the fantasy was crushed, her ego became fragile and swung to the opposite extreme. She engaged in "rescuing solutions" — running errands, doing favors, troubleshooting, lending money — in the vain hope that she could cure the ills of her lover, only to find that this monster man had turned against her.

We need to escape the Furies that follow us during most of our earthly life and put in perspective the psychological traumas of early childhood — abandonment, abuse, incest, emotional deprivation, lack of love. And we also need to escape from what is sometimes "normal" development in a society — casting women and men in specific roles and resolving conflicts in a manner determined by society. It is our human urge to seek *healing* in our current life.

The woman must cease seeking fulfillment in external resources and return to her inner, intricate self. Enough of this participation in committees and causes. It is time to put a stop to demands and distractions. Woman is still her own center, the axis of the wheel; no more centrifugal activities need to be added to her life. She must consciously encourage those pursuits that oppose the centrifugal forces of today. Women need quiet time alone for contemplation, prayer, music, reading, study, or work. The pursuit does not need to be earth-shaking, but it should express something of their own spontaneity, such as picking and arranging flowers.

At every moment of her life, a woman is bound by her own essential nature to pursue her transformation according to her inner destiny. Is she satisfied with her emotional, spiritual, and intellectual evolution? Has she synthesized her past and present perceptions of life? Is she in harmony with herself? She needs to reflect on herself and her life rather than pursue hobbies and distractions. She also needs to preserve energy and not permit it to be drained away by her job, family, and domestic life. If she has wrestled with her appearance, her body development, her physique, and the reduction of the extra pound, gray hair, and wrinkles, she may consider whether she has moved forward or become mired in some inhibiting point. Any dissatisfaction with her physical form, any cramped condition has a corresponding inner attitude. It is an indication that her psyche, as yet unrealized, is always absolute in its demand for fulfillment.

To pursue the realization of the psyche means forsaking the brilliance of the rational mind, the lure of what the externalities offer, and entering what may be called the semi-darkness of the soul to rediscover the essence of life. By relinquishing those fantasies that promise earthly paradise — the alluring voices of the advertisers — and by ridding herself of the frustration that follows, the voice of the soul will sound stronger.

For every woman there is a personal journey toward the development of all her emotional, mental, and spiritual faculties. She must speak out: "I am a human being. I must no longer be defined by roles. I believe in the primacy of the human being not conditioned by sex." Could there be a more beautiful message that she could convey?

It is her human choice to expect to be treated as a person and not as a *mere woman,* as simply a woman and only that. She could seek inspiration from strong female models, women who have changed history, who stand the test of time, the *eternal* female. She has the right to refuse to be identified with a certain image of a woman: the stars and starlets of mass media or fashion models, the exploited women of the advertising industry. All attitudes that limit the possibilities of women are mistaken. Women have the right to be respected and be on a parity with men.

Women have every reason to protest and to rise up against the longstanding prejudicial attitudes of society. But in the process, they can lose perspective. In an effort to be constructive, they can be destructive. For example, some women go to the extreme in current social issues. Rather than balancing and integrating their feminine energies with their masculine energies, they may virtually deny the feminine in themselves. A woman may reject traditional feminine roles in order to prove to men that she can play masculine roles. Here exists the danger of the masculinization of women. Ironically, this attitude can proceed from an unconscious evaluation of the masculine principle and masculine roles as inherently superior to feminine. There is no such inherent superiority. What is needed is an honoring and valuing of the feminine principle and the ways and roles through which this energy can be expressed by both men and women. Masculine roles are neither better nor worse than feminine roles. Both are needed and are of equal value.

The longing and restlessness of our heart and the urge of our psyche gradually make us aware of our bond with the world we live in, and then we realize what we are living is an extension of our old life, that is, a self defined by others including parents, teachers, peers — a self that is facing death. Once we realize that until now others have defined who we are, their definition of us can be changed. This is the creative moment, and here we need imagination and initiative. When we decide to take possession of that moment, our own reality, then we can move out of the complex societal pressures into a celebration of a life that we design. We can take a course in the local college, join an art class, attend gymnastics. Limitless possibilities exist if we can connect with philanthropic and educational institutions and offer our services or if we simply make an effort to connect with the world around us, our neighbors and friends.

We might arrive at the conclusion that the unhappiness of the ten couples referred to at the beginning of the chapter originated with the woman partner: "It's because of him that I'm unhappy." A therapist's task is to seek the root of all evil in the abyss of the unconscious rather than improvise temporary solutions. Frequently a woman experiences herself in a state of tension between two realities. First, there is the world of whims and fashions, which confines her to conformity and obligations of roles, endangers her existence, tempts her with promises and hopes of happiness, and demands her obedience. Second, there is her soul, the supernatural state of *being* hidden within her, her psyche, for which she yearns. This psyche ceaselessly calls her forth beyond the laws and boundaries of her little personal life to service of the Greater Life.

It is fortunate that none of the ten women acknowledged emotional, physical, or sexual abuse in their relationships — a fact that enabled this writing to focus mainly on the dissatisfaction. Consider psychological realities:

- We marry people who bear the characteristics of either or both our parents, because we seek familiarity.

- We marry our fantasies — "This person has all the qualities that I need in a spouse" — because nature lacks logic but seeks fulfillment.

- We pursue the other for completeness, because by ourselves we feel incomplete.

No matter what psychosocial realities propel us into heterosexual relationships, the female psyche experiences a void. She is innocently waiting for improvement in her life, perhaps expecting to meet an understanding man, trusting the law of reciprocity — someone, somewhere, somehow will respond to her efforts and appreciate her. The antidote to this state of suspension is self-determination, action, and movement.

If perfection belongs to God, then the search for completeness or wholeness is the most a human being can hope for in a relationship, marital or otherwise. Striving single-mindedly to find fulfillment with irrational foolishness — the idea that another person can fill the emptiness — is to miss many of the joys of living. If we seek perfection in our human interaction, in essence we exaggerate or isolate parts of ourselves, limiting our life to partial living, and consequently we become disappointed.

Like the mythical Andromeda chained to the rock, some women are conditioned to tolerate the chains of helplessness. Their authority is diminished to what they ought or ought not to do in the future, and to the "if only's" of the past. Life for them is ahead or behind but seldom here. They live expecting the unexpected, trying to change the world. If they receive from the outside what they want, temporarily they are happy; if not, they are forever unhappy. When playing with externalities, we delude ourselves into believing we are creating our own world. If we are fortunate enough to achieve the false goal of our fantasy, we may find ourselves alone with our models, bereft of what we most longed for in life: loving and being loved.

Since the purpose of this chapter is to offer hope and not to hurt feelings, consider the following.

Thoughts to Ponder

- Women, single or married, sister, wife, or lover: as you remodel your house or your room to match your needs today, feel free to redefine yourself. Become aware of what you are and what you are not, and pursue an image appropriate for you.

- The definition of you given by others — teachers, parents, peers, relatives, mass media — is not really accurate. Develop your own definition that describes you adequately.

- Once you redefine yourself as to who you are today, you may choose to cultivate your individuality. Your individuality cannot be your ideas or your fantasies or your "should" system.

- Live in dialogue with another person who is open-minded, honest, and willing to maintain the dialogue. You cannot be human unless you are speaking to another person. The absence of dialogue is emotional death.

- Do not expect all people to agree with you. They do not have to. You are the authority of your life but not the absolute authority: that is God's province.

- Be fully present in the immediacy of the moment. Whatever you are involved in, focus on it before you go to the next project. Most people live in the past or in the future but not in the present.

- Stop looking for external reasons to explain your unhappiness. If this instant is worthwhile, live it now. If it is not, then you need to move on to the next experience.

- Maturity occurs slowly. You can transcend yourself only in spurts. Live your potential creatively. Be the architect of your life. In your design, include the possibility of friendship. Find a good friend and develop an ongoing relationship.

- As you process your thoughts, choose the good part of you and use it. Do not choose to act on your fantasies, although some fantasies could become a motivating force in your life.

- Learn to accept your limitations. Test your reality instead of choosing grandiosity. If you cannot sing, do not pursue the idea of becoming an opera star. Perhaps you could learn to dance.

Chapter 16

From Conflict to Choice

> The normal conflict is concerned with an actual
> choice between two possibilities, both of which
> the person finds really desirable.
>
> —*Karen Horney*

Of course there is pain, injustice, cruelty in the world. You are probably in some conflict now, or you have had your share of pain. Perhaps you have been cheated; many times you have been hurt. Count the times if you wish. Then, think what change you can make to stop hurting. The suffering is a given, but the resolution of a problem, subjective and arbitrary as it may seem, rests finally upon nothing more than your will, upon your being able to say: "This is what I want to change."

Having had the opportunity to explore areas of male and female dissatisfactions, we now turn to improvise some alternatives. If all humans experience an existential feeling of dissatisfaction, we need to develop alternate choices to combat our discomfort and move on from conflict to choice.

What are these choices?

It is my impression that you are reading this book primarily because you would like to improve your present life. In view of the dissatisfactions that you personally experience, you would like to see yourself fulfilled, healthy, and happy. But, what holds you up? What blocks you?

Contrary to psychoanalytical precepts that attempt to trace our unhappiness to our early childhood experiences, I dare to point out that we fear our best as well as our worst, even though in different ways. There is no doubt that we all have unused potentialities or not fully developed ones. So often we run away from responsibilities. When we speak of assuming responsibility for the self, we mean the capacity to stand up for what we believe is right and a willingness to take the consequences if our action or decision should prove to be wrong. This, too, is difficult when a person is divided by conflicts.

We are generally afraid to become that which we can glimpse in our most perfect moments. Although we enjoy the god-like possibilities we see in ourselves in such moments, we simultaneously shiver with weakness, awe, and fear before these same possibilities. A great deal has been written about the fear of success. We can understand this fear. Success implies hard work, ability to respond, responsibility, awareness, commitment to the task at hand, and a healthy attitude. The absence of these qualities signals failure, and failure does not require much effort. You do not need to do anything. It comes on its own. At times we pretend that we do not know what action to take or we prefer not to know, because if we did know, then we would have to act and stick our neck out.

Some people are able to live a life of maximum health and good feeling. They look into themselves and take charge of all their good qualities and use them with full intensity. They make healthy choices. They do not focus on problems; they work on them to provide solutions. Of course they have problems. Everybody has to face reality-based problems: illness, inflation, job crises, unemployment, disappointing children, betrayal of love, infidelity of a mate, aging, death. The difference is that people who choose to live a life of maximum emotional and physical health develop a *different attitude* toward each problem. First, they recognize problems as a human condition. They do not even use the term "problems." They prefer to call them "issues" to be resolved. Second, they do not measure happiness by the absence of problems but maintain themselves as worthy and happy people in spite of the anxieties of life. When they meet with difficulties, instead of becoming troubled or blaming others for their fate, they analyze *how* they view life.

There are as many successful ways of living as there are lives to be lived, and all that can be done is to encourage others to live full and courageous lives within the framework that they have made for themselves.

Perhaps at one time or another you have admired or even envied successful people. Personally, I admire those who represent the true, the good, the beautiful, the just, the men and women who are creative or endowed with a great intellect. However, in their presence, I feel uneasy; a tinge of jealousy permeates my thinking, and I ignore my own self-worth temporarily. As I become aware of my feelings and accept who I am, I fend off my jealousy and learn to love more purely the good qualities in others. This makes me appreciate whatever good qualities I possess. Just as beauty is in the eye of the beholder — that is, we must first possess beauty ourselves inwardly in order to behold it — so it is with all other attributes. Appreciation of others is also a tribute to oneself. Knowing this eliminates envy and useless comparisons.

During this reading, you may suddenly decide to stop looking at and evaluating the possessions of others. You may take a brief inventory of what good qualities *you* possess, such as being good-hearted, generous, responsible, and willing to work. As you enumerate these qualities, your old habits may surface to stifle your good intentions. These must be replaced by new values that you can steadily learn to develop. In comparing these new values to your old habits, you will experience a sense of guilt. "Why did I not do what I should have done?" This sort of guilt is a cry of the self for healing and development. What you were not able to do for yourself is now history, no longer within your control. What you plan to do today and during the immediate tomorrow is your choice.

You have a body and a psyche. These two components interrelate, and one cannot exist without the other. However, they affect each other: emotions/feelings affect bodily functions, and bodily functions affect our spirit. The same person can love and hate, perhaps not at the same exact moment. Yet, there is no love without a tinge of hate, and no hate without at least some attraction. As we mature, we come to accept and enjoy life with this kind of ambiguity. It is difficult, but not necessary, to hold love and hate in a creative tension, to recognize that both can be right and both can be wrong, depending on what we are trying to accomplish. We can be sure that love is a creative energy. Hate is a destructive force.

We are fully aware of the time and money invested for the exploration of outer space. We marvel at the ability of our scientists to send spaceships around the earth, to the moon and back. Medical science has made spectacular progress in correcting deformities of the body, performing transplants, and providing intricate surgical interventions. While such scientific explorations excite the mind, they do not seem to do much for the suffering soul. We have too many unhappy, emotionally disturbed people who are unable to find comfort, peace, and joy.

In the age of rapid change and insecurity, individuals and families are undergoing significant transformations. Changes in lifestyles, passionate self-scrutiny, turbulent family interaction, conflicts in values, competitive feelings, undefined or even unrealistic expectations confuse the mind and frustrate any attempt to create a meaningful way of life. We may have attained intellectual success, yet we experience a feeling of emptiness, an emotional deprivation. Often enough, the more we learn about ourselves, the less we think of ourselves. The more we observe life, the less we participate in living.

Living as God meant us to live requires that we understand and appreciate what is ours — our humanity. We develop our bodies and find them strong, beautiful, and useful. We cultivate our minds and find them God's greatest gift to humans when used creatively. We are truthful, honest with ourselves and others. We are willing to take risks, to change when the situation calls for it, to hold back if what is ahead seems dangerous. We adjust to what is new and different, keeping what is useful and discarding what is not. Doing these things makes us healthy, alert, sensitive, playful, loving, and productive human beings.

To live optimally as human beings, it is important to explore some of our basic human needs. What are they?

Love. This feeling of being wanted and cared for is one of the most central issues of life. Infants separated from their homes and placed in institutions where they are well taken care of as far as their physical needs are concerned, yet who are emotionally neglected, may become apathetic and *often die.* If you have experienced a great deal of love in early childhood, you are a lucky person. You do have self-confidence; you feel an inner peace. As a result, you seek the company of loving people and you will find a mate who can love and enjoy life.

Persons who grew up in a loveless environment are forever thirsty; they seek companions who cannot love, and ultimately they feel rejected. Such people have a hard time loving anyone, including themselves.

Sex. This sacred and significant aspect of the human personality tends to be the Gordian knot of human interaction. People probably differ more in their actual desire and means of obtaining satisfaction than in any other need. The ability and wish to have sexual satisfaction is observed even in infants. To be frustrated in this need is an invitation to anger, distractibility, and reduced self-esteem. The shaping of the sexual response is subjected to all kinds of pressures from the family, school, community, mass media, and religion. Some individuals cannot accept their sexuality at all; others set up very rigid constraints before they permit themselves to experience sex. Still others see sex as the most important determinant of their happiness.

Security. As deceiving as the word "security" can be, most of us need to have someone trustworthy who cares for us and will patch up our wounds. A mother gives this type of security to her helpless infant. But if "mothering-fathering" is absent because of death or divorce or long-term illness, the child becomes excessively insecure and dependent on his or her own resources for survival. Lack of security causes withdrawal. A person who feels insecure will look for relationships in which dependency is the most important consideration, or the person may avoid people and intimacy to a large extent in order not to be left alone again.

Recognition. Apart from belonging to a family, it is important for us to belong to other groups — an organization, a church, a temple, a system — where we feel we are valued and are able to make a contribution. For some people, the idea of being part of a family — that is, as the father or mother — is extremely important. Our immigrant ancestors integrated their drives into productivity, to make something valuable for themselves, their families, and their new homeland. We all appreciate the contributions of the immigrants that have profoundly influenced their successors. It is one of the healthiest components of a happy life to be creatively productive in one's occupation, marriage, or social life. Others find satisfaction in being part of a large organization, for example, a big company, an educational institution, or one of the armed forces. Still others attach themselves to an important individual and vicariously experience a sense of greatness and recognition.

Companionship. You may be a part of a crowd and still feel lonely. Loneliness is experienced by many people as the most feared state of mind. Unless there is somebody *there for them,* they become extremely troubled, unable to function, and likely to make poor decisions in a variety of areas. When we belong to a group we feel validated, and not only can we develop the courage to appreciate this group, but also we can actively and joyfully participate in it. We can try to do things that are satisfying or new or creative.

Curiosity. The quest for newness can be a most interesting and satisfying part of life. This drive has taken our technology into outer space. This is also the drive for *meaning,* for understanding of our environment and ourselves. How little we understand and how little interest we have in knowing and getting to the bottom of things. We get bored, and boredom is slothfulness. The world is full of mystery to be explored and cherished. You can imagine developing a sense of curiosity for your personal growth, reading books, attending courses or lectures, socializing, and learning from others.

Power. You must have heard the expression, Power corrupts, and absolute power corrupts absolutely. History is a sad commentary on political and religious leaders who tried to control and subjugate various peoples. The drive for power and superiority emerges from our inferiority complex. Frequently we develop the goal of overcoming weakness through being superior to others. Alfred Adler warns, however, in *What Life Should Mean to You,* that while the striving for superiority is behind every human creation, the only individuals who can really meet the problems of life are those who show in their striving a tendency to enrich all others.

Growth. Abraham Maslow's concept of *self-actualization* refers to the capacity to be spontaneous, to be expressive, to see reality without reference to one's own needs, to create, to identify with many others. Individuals with a drive toward growth extend their personalities and experiences in a variety of ways without neurotic fear of the consequences. Growth implies change, but change is frightening. It requires courage and determination to become all that we can be. It is an ongoing struggle to overcome passivity, procrastination, and victimization.

Once we estimate realistically our good qualities and leave behind the bad ones, then we apply self-discipline to improve our sense of self-esteem, and, finally, we select a goal that is within our grasp and pursue it. We do have the tools.

Thoughts to Ponder

- Observe how the mischief monger, your past, tries to hurt. Can you afford the time and energy needed to ruminate on your unfortunate childhood? All humans are victimized by their past hurts.

- When you feel stress or you experience anxiety, do you need to be a helpless victim of symptoms? Or could you examine your thoughts about what is going on in your life?

- If you are unable to resolve your tension entirely through self-observation, could you involve yourself in activities — swimming, jogging, walking, bird-watching, volunteer work — that could diffuse your tension, even temporarily?

- Have you met anyone in your lifetime who obtained total gratification of all of his or her needs? Could you still experience joy if only a small portion of your needs were satisfied, or do you prefer to wait until you have all that you want?

- Is there some way that you could trace the origin of your dissatisfaction? Once you get a clue, you will not feel so helpless since you will have some awareness about its origins. Then you will be in a better position to do things to correct your dissatisfaction. If you apply yourself a little bit every day you can do much to rectify matters.

- Life can be painful, often unbearably unfair and unjust, but it is seldom tragic. We go through traumatic events, we have dramatic episodes, but they are not totally catastrophic. You may have fallen in love or out of love. You may have lost a loved one. It is important *how* you experience yourself *now*, and what you decide to do at this hour.

Chapter 17

Meet Mr. T., a Man Who Changed

> All changes, even the most longed for, have their
> melancholy; for what we leave behind us is a part
> of ourselves; we must die to one life before we
> can enter into another.
>
> —*Anatole France*

I met Tony T. seven years ago when he had just been released
from state prison. "For something stupid I did," said Tony. "I've
learned a lesson. I've changed." He sighed and smiled.

In his eyes, I saw pain. In his face, I saw a man who went
through the torments of prison life for three years and survived.
He looked older than his thirty-three years.

"I know you write books. I want you to write about my life
in prison," he said seriously.

"I would rather write about your *change*," I said.

"Why?"

"Your example of change confirms my convictions that
people change because they want to," I said, "not because a
therapist or an external authority imposes a change on them."

"I changed because I decided to change," said Tony, and
after that sentence, I switched on the tape recorder, and the
documentation of his change began:

It was hard to adjust to the light. Prison was terribly dark.
However, the hardest part was adjusting to the people. I walked
around with such fear in my heart that I became paranoid. What
if someone stuck a knife in my back? My loving wife, Carol, was

172

compassionate. She, too, has survived three years of questions and malicious gossip about my case.

Now that I am out of prison, I am free to choose how I will spend each minute. I can be creative. I don't fit into any role definition. I can take any job and do well in it. I cannot waste time complaining or wishing that things were otherwise. I'm enthusiastic about being alive and know that I can get out of life whatever is possible.

Every morning I take a walk and enjoy nature around me. I walk in the rain and get the thrill out of feeling raindrops on my face. In snow, I delight at the sound my shoes make. I cannot think of anything I dislike doing. I like life. I like cats, dogs, and birds. Rats, snakes, and mosquitoes I can do without.

Mistakes? I make many, but I try to avoid repeating them. I refuse to harbor guilt and shame for my former life. I no longer have control over my yesterdays. No amount of guilt and shame can change the past. My attitude has changed and I have learned a great deal about what not to do.

I no longer worry about the past, and I'm careful not to worry about the future. I have no control over the next hour. Anything can happen, good or bad. How can I worry about the future? As I live my life in the present, I make basic plans for tomorrow, so when tomorrow comes, I will not be in want. I get every pleasure possible out of my daily life.

When I decide to do something, I don't postpone it and wish for a better opportunity. I just go ahead and do it. Procrastination is hidden calculation waiting for an undefined pay-off, and it results in passivity.

I have a strong love for my wife and am devoted to her. She is my best friend and partner. I also have a few friends that I deeply respect. In these relationships, I feel independent. I respect my wife and my friends, but I don't cling to them. My love implies no imposition on their values. I know my boundaries, and I allow them to cherish theirs. My wife likes to be alone at times, and I go to great lengths to ensure that such privacy is protected.

We socialize with a number of people, but our friends deserve exclusivity. We are selective about our love and those we love are few. When it comes to helping others, we are careful not to encourage dependency upon us. We help people to foster a sense of independence in themselves. Personally, I love those who love to be independent, to make their own choices, and to live their lives for themselves. I cannot waste my time blaming my parents or those who have wronged me in the past. I cannot blame my addiction to alcohol on my peers or on my environment. I chose it as my companion to escape reality. Nothing that happened and nothing that anyone did to me is to blame for what I did. What I did came out of my mistaken notion of what life ought to be according to my imagination.

What others think of me is of no consequence to me. As my grandfather used to say, "The advice of many people makes a person crazy." I don't want anyone's approval. I don't need anybody's applause or praise. When someone speaks against me or disapproves of what I do, I process that person's comments, and if I don't like the person, I try not to harbor him or her in my mind. I don't need to be loved by everyone.

I'm not very well educated, but I'm what they call streetwise. I read a lot. When I talk to people who are educated, I cherish their learning and try not to interrupt. Although I see education and culture as important aspects of life, I refuse to be ruled by them.

I enjoy funny stories and like to repeat them, adding my own gusto to them. I love to see people laugh. People with stony faces I avoid. Smilers I join and make them laugh. I'm sensitive to sarcasm; it's a form of hostility. Never will I use ridicule as a means of creating laughter. I don't laugh at people; I laugh with them.

Appearances do not impress me. I maintain the thought that it is not only fine feathers that make fine birds. I accept people as they are. If they are different from me, I don't feel offended by their presence. Artificialities I avoid. I don't even like artificial flowers.

I accept myself and the world around me, and I make a daily effort to adjust to life without groaning and moaning that life should be different. While I'm grateful to be alive, I realize that whatever changes need to be made for my welfare, I will have to make them myself.

This is the part of Tony's story that concerns us. Tony's experience is evidence of human potential. Does that mean we should all go to jail for three years? Certainly not, any more than that we should all travel to outer space. Examples of self-rediscovery and change do help to support the potential that is part of our humanity.

For many people, suffering is imposed; there is no escape. It may be impersonal and unavoidable, like fire, flood, and cancer, or it may be man-made, like riots, wars, sack of cities, domestic violence, incest, rape. Do such victims have a choice? A dim ray of hope exists for them. They may bow in prayer; they may curse or plead; but they may not choose to suffer or not to suffer. That choice has been foreclosed. Starving blacks in Somalia scrounge for roots and fight each other for gazelles. African children with swollen bellies and emaciated bodies wander homeless, hungry, and orphaned across a lunar desert.

In the land of plenty, many of us have never known this kind of misery, and yet we suffer too as we witness it through the media. Wealth and intelligence and good fortune are no guarantees of protection. Misery comes equally to all, but the degree differs. Some of our suffering is altogether private, known to no one but the sufferer. Suffering is part of being human. There are a few tranquil ones who have little conflict, and they suffer less; at the other extreme are those who go berserk, stretched by despair to the breaking point. In between are the rest of us, not miserable enough to go mad or jump off a bridge, and yet, if we are honest, unable to admit that we have come to terms with life, are at peace with ourselves, and are happy. If suffering is part of the human condition and we are subjected to it, what can we do to bring about *a change?* Trees, plants, flowers, and animals reach their potential on their own. A human being needs to move on, to practice ceaselessly the tasks of growth. We need to make ourselves aware of what the truth is about us and what the desirable changes are that we would like to accomplish.

If we emulate the leopard who cannot change his spots and say, "That's the way I am, and I might as well accept it," we abandon the choice to change and to exploit what we have been in the past, and thus we avoid responsibility for what we shall be in the future.

Often we do not choose to take a new direction and find ourselves drifting into those old modes that eventually define us: Ill-fated me. Nobody cares. What's the use? We did not choose to be what we have become, but gradually, imperceptibly, became what we are by drifting into doing those things we now characteristically do.

The most common illusion of therapy-seekers and, strangely, even of experienced therapists, is that *change* can take place in a therapeutic environment. The most common disappointment of therapy is that it does not automatically make the change. Insights, correct interpretations, skillful analyses, and the presence of an empathic therapist: all of these are instruments for making change and are essential components of the process, but they do not directly achieve the change. Some sufferers do not want to change. They make their presence known in life by suffering. More often it is the *not doing*, a state of passivity, that sets us adrift.

An anguished woman entered my office, sat down, and wept. She began to talk and I listened. A married man whom she had loved with a passion for seven years had returned to his wife and family. She was heart-broken, for she had built high hopes, and he had led her on with promises that some day they would have a life together. It is not an uncommon story.

I looked at her with compassion, as if I knew what the problem *really* was and what we would do about it. The theories I had learned about the suffering soul were of no value. If I were to take a profound look into the jungle of her misery, I knew I would get lost. What did I have to work with? Perhaps hope? Hope for a possible change. Maybe that would be enough.

The suffering is a given, but the problem is a choice. It is subjective and arbitrary and rests finally upon nothing more than the person's will, the power of making a reasoned choice, the enthusiasm and energy for being able to say, "This is what I want to change."

Personality change follows change in behavior. Since we are what we do, if we want to change what we are, we must begin by changing what we do; we must undertake a new mode of action. At first, the new mode will be experienced as difficult, unpleasant, forced, unnatural, anxiety-provoking. It may have to be undertaken lightly, but it can only be sustained by a considerable effort of will. Change will occur only if such action is maintained over a long period of time.

To build a house an architect and a contractor, a blueprint and material are essential, as well as the finances. In building the house of our life or in its remodelling, we may delegate nothing, for if the task is to be accomplished, it can only be done in the workshop of our own mind and heart, in the most intimate rooms of thinking and feeling where none but our self has freedom of movement or competence or authority. The responsibility lies with the sufferer, originates with that person, and remains with that person to the end. Whether the *change* takes place in or out of a therapy room, with or without a therapist, the individual bears the whole responsibility.

If inner forces beyond a person's consciousness continue to resist a desirable change and the process of change comes to a halt, a therapist may help, perhaps crucially. However, a therapist's best help will be of no avail if he or she is expected to provide a kind of insight that will of itself achieve change. There is no short-cut, no safe conduct, no easy way. Our destiny is shaped from within.

The process of change that originates in our heart and expands outward, always within the purview and direction of a knowing consciousness, begins with a vision of freedom, an "I-want-to-become" attitude with a sense of the potentiality to become what we are not. We grope toward this vision in the dark, with no guide, no map, and no guarantee. Here we act as subject, author, creator.

More often than not, the course toward a change entails anxiety, uncertainty, and confusion, so that reappraisal becomes necessary. We find that the entire self was not known, that submerged aspects of the self now rise up in terror, threaten, and demand revocation. We are forced to a halt, sometimes driven back. The whole issue needs to be rethought. "Maybe I don't want to change. Am I going at it the wrong way?" Here therapy may offer insight into the bewildering experience, help with the making of new connections, give comfort and encouragement, assist in the always slippery decision of whether to hang on and try harder or look for a different approach.

Sometimes we suffer desperately and would try anything that would find us some relief, but we feel lost, we find no way, and the outlook seems hopeless. We take a personal inventory and find no connection between the misery we experience and the way we live. The pain and frustration come from somewhere, but we have no clue to follow. We are bored, nothing makes sense, life has no meaning, and we become depressed. Something is wrong, but we cannot imagine another way of living that would free us from suffering. *What can we do?*

If the suffering is serious and intractable, it must be intimately and extensively connected, in ways we do not perceive, with the way we live. We have to look for such connections. Sometimes there is nothing to be done until the source of the suffering is found. If we find the connections, we may begin to see how a change in the way we live will make for a change in the way we feel.

There is a time when things may get worse. "Things get worse before they get better." You have heard this before. You may not be able to keep what you have; you must incorporate loss. Instability may be part of your life. Uncertainty. You may be bewildered and dismayed. Things may not meet your expectations. You may find in yourself a sense of apathy, of pervading pessimism and sadness. You may find yourself stuck, unable to disconnect from your past. Be alert to those situations in which you find yourself discouraged or depressed, in which you are embarrassed or anxious, and in which you are taken by surprise. These are great signs that you are in a situation where you have unparalleled opportunity for personal growth. Discouragement, depression, and anxiety may present you with extraordinary opportunities. Out of every crisis comes wisdom, claims a Chinese proverb. Out of trouble comes direction. We need to be vigilant. In a confused and unsettled time, let us set ourselves firmly on the side of life, on the side of health. I know it is a hard commitment to make, but it is the only healthy way of life.

There is one indispensable requirement for this process of self-restoration, and that is openness. Most people are not open to themselves. In other words, the connection to our reality must not be just a power line; it must also be a communication link, a vital line of intercommunication. Openness in this sense means the awareness and recognition of what is happening to us, now. If we are feeling pain, we should not be afraid to admit it. The same, obviously, applies to grief or happiness, to tenderness and love, to feelings of confusion, conflict, and guilt. If communication is blocked, if we try to shut these things out of our consciousness, it does not mean they do not exist. It merely means we have not dealt with them. They will come back to haunt us. It goes without saying that we need to maintain similar connections to the world outside as well as the world within.

If we are open to ourselves and deal realistically with our life experiences, when we look self-confidently within, we have no need to distort what we see. When we are wanting in this vital self-knowledge, we are afraid to look inside, or when we do, we try to revise and reshape, in effect, to distort what we see. There is nothing sadder or ultimately more damaging than self-delusion. Whether we develop and possess this knowledge of self naturally or have to work at it, it is absolutely basic equipment for the job of self renewal. *Know thyself* — the ancient Greeks regarded it as the highest virtue. This is the only self we have. How can we hope to live with it, let alone live with it gracefully and happily, if we have a blurred and twisted perception of it? How can we ever know its vulnerabilities and its strengths? How can we ever know its failings and possibilities?

The restoration of the self in us is a lifelong process. It is within our power to begin now to move out of our present state of being. By the simple affirmation of our will to be, we can turn away from misery, dishonesty, meanness of spirit, prejudice, narrowness of mind, and faintness of heart; we can turn toward self-esteem, intellectual and aesthetic growth, self-love and other-love, and the acceptance of our own nature, not for what it is or has been, but for what it has the power to become — by the grace of the inner goodness that resides there and our earnest effort.

When we decide to change our ways, we inevitably undergo a sort of self-reconstruction, a sort of rebirth. The builder feels reborn among tools and materials. The physicist is eventually born anew into a world of atoms and particles. The medical researcher is born anew into a world of white corpuscles and hemoglobin and DNA. An athlete is born anew in the stadium, dressed in colorful uniform and ready for action in front of thousands of cheering spectators. Human beings must be born anew if they are going to achieve a meaningful realization of their own potential.

We cannot delude ourselves that we can remain passive and good things will happen in our life. We have to move toward something new and different. "Trust in movement," claimed Alfred Adler. "See what happens — not what you feel should or ought to happen in a situation." Adler was deeply aware that life happens at the level of events, not of words, and is always outside our ability to grasp it intellectually. Our body cannot stand up and sit down simultaneously. Each movement either follows a clear command of our own initiative, or we move at the initiative of another person. We must be constantly aware of whether we are initiating our action or taking direction from outside.

We cannot change the world except to the extent we change ourselves. It is our move. We cannot change other people. They are as they are. At best, we can model a good example. We can change ourselves; however, we can change *only* to the degree that we alter, modify, or become aware of our unrealistic expectations of what-should-be. It is *what-should-be* that bars the gate to reality.

Consider the lowly caterpillar. It is evident that the caterpillar and the butterfly live in entirely different worlds, and no one would ever say that a caterpillar is a butterfly or that a butterfly is a caterpillar. Yet we know that the caterpillar and the butterfly are simply different levels of expression of one entity. The caterpillar *can* fly, but not as a caterpillar — only as a butterfly. The caterpillar has the potential to fly, but something has to happen to accomplish this. We can do things that are desirable and beneficial, but not in our present condition. We must change. Only when we are *born anew* into a higher state of consciousness can we achieve our goals.

A caterpillar looked up and saw a colorful butterfly flitting among the flowers. He shook his head ruefully and said, "They will never get me in one of those contraptions." That's true; they never will. The caterpillar just cannot fly. Yet as the caterpillar changes its state, it enters a new world. Suddenly, there is a whole new set of principles at work, and it realizes a whole new potentiality.

Humans are caught in all sorts of limitations: unemployment, poverty, disease, privation. In a state of impasse, we view the lives of other people as spectacular, beyond duplication. They have all the luck and we have all the misery. Regardless of what evaluation we may make of our lives from our current condition, there is something in us that transcends the human.

Our human level of evaluation tells us that we cannot make a butterfly out of a caterpillar. Furthermore, we cannot make a criminal into a saint. But in a way beyond knowing, the caterpillar in the cocoon breaks loose into a winged colorful creature of the air. The criminal suddenly sees a new potential within and begins to act upon that potential. Becoming aware of this potential within, we see things in a different light, we react to a different set of principles, and we are free to do unlimited things.

In one of his most lucid moments, Henry Thoreau stated: "If one advances confidently in the direction of his dreams, and endeavors to live the life which he has imagined, he will meet with success unexpected in common hours."

Thoughts to Ponder

- Change is an ongoing activity of the body, mind, and soul, a normal function in human development. Not to change is not to develop. Change, which is constant, can be complex and thus, sometimes disquieting. However, the emerging forces from within us follow natural *laws*. They are governed and conditioned by the forces in our environment that they remain homeostatic, which is a fancy way of saying *in balance*.

- The emotional self is an integral part of the totality of the human organism, both forming it and being formed by it. What is experienced outwardly is simultaneously experienced inwardly. In the constant effort to achieve a healthier emotional climate, the inner self must be vigilantly in charge, making suitable allowances for what is happening externally.

- There is a creative process that relates the restored self to the totality of the personality. The same creative dynamic that molds and shapes the totality of the human being it forms also shapes and integrates us into the larger totality that is our world.

- Each person is a unique and distinctive human being. Each of us will and should, therefore, function at our own pace, in our own style, and according to our own convictions. Starting with the rudiments, we will, as we build confidence and gain greater self-knowledge, handle issues of more complexity and depth.

- We each have our own internal system for assimilating life experiences, rather in the way a tree draws from the earth and the air and the sun and by a process of photosynthesis converts these into enriching elements in its life. This is how we grow from modest beginnings and then branch out to encompass a rich variety of life experiences.

• When we are comfortable with the changes that we have set in motion, in other words, when we accept ourselves, the environment will likewise accept us, returning our self-confidence with its own respect. This might be called "psychic reciprocity." It is a simple but crucial law. The more positively we integrate with the life around us, contributing creatively to it, the more positive will be its response. Some people integrate totally without effect, contributing nothing, and of course getting nothing in return. Others integrate negatively, drawing on the resources of the societal "bank," but investing none of themselves. Life does not accept these terms any more than does the local bank. Sooner or later, people around us will cast off this dead weight.

• Whatever the initial results of self-reconstruction, we have left the static condition and have set in motion a dynamic force. We must go on exploring new and better ways to relate to the whole. If we are still limited in sensitivity and skill, the more likely we are to seek integration too abruptly and then be disappointed when the world is not quite ready to recognize our renewed self at face value. The more flexible and open and resilient we are, the greater will be our chances of relating to the whole with grace and ease, accepting other lifestyles for what they are, without judging, and, in turn, being accepted for what we are.

Chapter 18

Spirituality: A Tool or an Obstacle?

> The spiritual life is...part of the human
> essence. It is a defining characteristic of human
> nature...without which human nature is not
> fully human.
>
> —*Abraham Maslow*

"Spirituality scares me," says Frank Pittman, M.D., of Atlanta. "I am constantly wrestling with powers I can't see, taste, hear, or smell. And the more mysterious these powers, the more they leave me feeling weak and helpless and vulnerable....People are always trying to find the meaning of life. Religion serves that function. Religion tries to define the relationship of the individual with the universe. When religion works, it makes you feel personally connected to the powers of the universe and to everything in it. It makes you feel that you have been created to be as you are supposed to be, and so has everyone else. It's a nice sense of personal wholeness and world order. When you come to see yourself as part of something bigger than yourself, you feel you belong, you feel comfort and relief, and you feel goodwill toward the fellow members of your group."

There is a trend in our times for spirituality to creep into a therapist's office and gain a respectable focus for scientific research. While Freud dismissed religion as little more than a neurotic illusion, the emerging wisdom in psychology is that at least some varieties of religious experience are beneficial for mental health.

Some of the research confirms what programs like Alcoholics Anonymous have long taken as a tenet of faith, namely, that compelling belief improves mental health and is especially helpful to those who are tempted to harm themselves; and strong belief is also supportive in the organizing of one's life in terms of what matters and what does not. The emerging consensus among psychologists studying religion is that the spiritual life is more often of psychological benefit than not, and that it is time for a scientific look at religion that does more than dismiss it.

Carl G. Jung dismissed Freud's pathologizing of religion. In his book *Modern Man in Search of a Soul*, he wrote, "Religions are so near to the human soul that psychology least of all can afford to overlook them." In 1931, Jung stated: "Religions are psychotherapeutic systems in the most actual meaning of the word, and in the widest measure, and no matter what the world thinks about religious experience, the one who has it, possesses the great treasure of a thing that has provided him with the source of life, meaning and beauty, and that has given a new splendor to the world and to mankind."

Psychiatrist Smiley Blanton and the Rev. Norman Vincent Peale did much to bring psychiatry and religion into a working relationship. It makes sense that religion and psychology — each of which is concerned with the fullness of the human experience — should be recognized as partners because they function as partners within the human psyche.

Psychiatrist M. Scott Peck, in his best-seller *The Road Less Traveled*, has made a significant contribution to integrating the psychological and the spiritual. Also, many moral theologians today have made a further contribution by integrating the spiritual with the psychological as a help to understanding many moral dilemmas.

These two dimensions may be thought of as the psychological and spiritual eyes of the human person, which complement each other. One serves the other in the perception of a total view of life and of oneself. But if one eye is not functioning properly or is closed, it is difficult to get a realistic perception of life and an understanding of the human personality. If healthy, the two eyes assist us in forming a more holistic view of the person.

In a *Newsweek* article, "Talking to God," sociologist-novelist-priest Andrew M. Greeley claims that recent research indicates that more than three-quarters (78 percent) of all Americans pray at least once a week, and more than half (57 percent) report praying at least once a day. Even among atheists and agnostics, nearly one in seven (13 percent) still pray daily.

Two of my best friends claim to be atheists. They refuse to enter a church or a temple, except for a funeral of a friend. They do not believe in God. They do not pray; they do not feel that prayer is of any value. I doubt if either of them knows what it means to pray. Yet both are good, caring, honest, and loving men. They are sensitive to the needs of others, generous with their time, wise with admonitions and love. On the other hand, we all know people who are always involved in church or temple activities and continuously invoke the name of God in their conversations. But when it comes to dealing with other people, they turn out to be of low tolerance, judgmental, insecure, quick to find fault, and eager to pronounce sentence.

Most people resort to prayer in times of crisis — when their child is ill with an incurable disease, when death is near for a parent or a spouse, or when every means has been exhausted without results. But those who pray only at such moments usually experience great difficulty figuring out what they are supposed to say and whom they are addressing.

Petitioning God for favors is one of the oldest — and most human — forms of prayer. In the Gospel of St. John, Jesus himself promised his disciples that "whatsoever you ask the Father in my name will be given to you." Most Americans who pray believe that at least some of their prayers have been answered, though not always in the ways in which the petitioners have sought.

Clearly, there is a difference between turning to God for help and expecting God to meet our every want. Jesus' own prayer to the Father was "Thy will be done" — meaning that God wants whatever promotes our participation in the divine life.

In essence, prayer — communing with God — is a journey with God as well as toward God, a journey in which prayer becomes, for those who pursue it, as natural as breathing.

Orthodox Christianity praises prayer that pertains to whatever is good and beneficial to the soul, "for the safekeeping of the inner spirit."

At the time of my training in therapy some twenty years ago, the mention of God, prayer, or a religious interest caused most psychologists to dismiss these topics with a quiet lift of the eyebrow. The implication, although not verbal, was that they were an indication of immaturity or some form of neurosis.

At the same time, theologians, insecure in their own belief systems, were arrogant. Psychotherapy, they thought, increased preoccupation with a "self" that they believed was a fiction.

Both religion and psychology seemed very sure of their superior ability to engineer human development and change, and at the same time each was unwilling to admit to any common ground. The result was an underground rivalry. "Psychotherapy and religion are in direct ideological competition," said long-time critic of psychiatry Thomas Szasz. "Psychotherapy is not different in any way from religion. Psychotherapy deals with how one should live, with self, family life, sexual behavior, and the purpose of life — and that's what religion is all about."

It is beyond doubt that God and religion have been misused both to the advantage of the hierarchy and to the disadvantage of the believer. Spirituality is often used as a cop-out, a way of avoiding responsibility for one's life, negating one's potential, and attributing every initiative to God. Unable to face the reality of death, unwilling to accept that what we do hurts those whom we do not intend to hurt, that we do not live up to our own potential, we can easily interpret these painful realities as God's will.

In spite of the drawbacks, we can still ask pertinent questions: Can therapy ever replace what sound religion can provide? Can a therapist's office, with its diploma-lined and art-decorated walls, replace the simplest church or temple? Religion provides a sense of community, connection with something beyond ourselves, a fellowship of people who share in a common faith, help freely given, and a broad view of suffering as inevitable and part of the human condition in which believers search for meaning. In the past, only a few therapists secretly sought spirituality for themselves, realizing that the principles of psychotherapy were insufficient to provide them with guidance for a more profound level of self-exploration. Those who discovered some value in spirituality did not feel comfortable enough to recommend it to their clients.

One cannot deny the fact of healing that has been experienced by many people who sought help in their respective faiths. Miracles have occurred over and over again to people who believed. There is not much publicity given to them, because the ones who experience miraculous healing are humble folks who do not advertise. Simply, they believe.

Each person is a psychological and spiritual being, although the spiritual dimension is frequently not recognized or not developed. To stress one dimension and disregard the other is to limit the understanding of both. The search for meaning and healing in our lives, our ability to function in a fully human way, occurs in both parts as one influences the other. In the climate of moral confusion today, where values and ideals are negated, many human problems have a deep spiritual dimension, and many psychological disorders will find genuine healing only within the context of the spiritual dimension.

The danger of relying on spiritual approaches is that they can lead to a sentimental hope that a sense of connection to a larger system will take away the pain of being a human being, or that the spiritual will be a substitute for what must be done on a psychological level by oneself. Although the spiritual and the psychological realms may overlap, they are not identical, and both are important.

Frequently, religious ignorance or neurotic religious views sabotage our spiritual dimension. Instead of bringing healing, distorted religious truths aggravate our problems, causing confusion and anger.

Spirituality means an ongoing connection with the ultimate reality called God. It is a belief that in all our problems God is present within us. This awareness is not presumption that God will miraculously remove our problems and cure all our ills. It is an inner conviction that God will lead us through our dark valleys, supporting and strengthening us on the way. We can also keep in mind that out of critical situations comes direction. A confidence in God engenders confidence in ourselves as we deal with difficulties. This faith endows us with the potential to manage our lives if only we use it. If we can grasp the idea of our spiritual dimension, we will find a deeper meaning in our lives and in our problems, and we will be more in charge of our destiny and safekeeping.

"Spirituality" derives from the word "spirit," not a child's white-sheeted ghost flying around, but an inner energy, creative choice, and a powerful force for living. It is connected with a Power greater than ourselves, a co-creatorship with God that allows us to be guided by God and yet to take responsibility for our lives. We diminish our ability to be positive and creative human beings if we expect God to do our work while we remain in a state of inertia; so it is in psychotherapy. We can make things happen; we create the difference, not in our old dysfunctional pattern of isolated control, but in choosing a partnership with our Higher Power — however we define that entity. Once we make the choice, the miracle is possible. Integrating spirituality in our lives requires faith in a reality that our physical eyes cannot see. What if we truly believed there is a God, a beneficent power that creates and keeps things together without our conscious control? What if we started observing that force working in our daily lives? What if we believed it loved us and cared for us and protected us? Think about it for a precious moment, and then touch and feel your body and become aware of its functions: an array of mechanisms with a brilliance of design and efficiency our human efforts have never begun to match. Our hearts beat, our lungs breathe, our ears hear, our hair grows, and we do not have to do anything to make them work — they just do. Planets revolve around the sun, seeds become flowers, embryos become babies — all with no help from us. We are parts of the system controlled by that force. We can let our lives be directed by the same endowment that makes the universe function, or we can do it ourselves. To trust in life's inherent order and harmony — that is faith in the presence of that force.

Faith is the beginning of spirituality. It is a surrender to something bigger than ourselves: to God who knows creation. When we stop trying to control events, they fall into a natural order, an order led by God. We are at peace while a power much greater than ours takes over, and it does a much better job than we can do. We learn to trust that power that holds galaxies together, that can handle the circumstances of our relatively little lives. When we surrender to our soul we let go of our attachment to how things happen on the outside and we become more concerned with what happens on the inside. Until we make that choice, we keep striving for results we may never attain. Money, sex, power, or any other worldly satisfactions offer temporary relief but not real joy. They are put into perspective rather than discarded.

How can I live in a world marked by fear, hatred, and violence, feeling hurt and betrayed, and still make sense of my life? Many people have asked this question and searched for an answer. Is there an answer?

Hardly a day passes in our lives without our experience of inner insecurities, fears, anxieties, apprehensions, and preoccupations with things over which we have no control. It seems that unseen dark powers pervade every part of our world to such an extent that we can never fully escape them. Still, it is possible not to belong to these controlling forces, not to build our dwelling place among them, but rather to make different choices.

One of these choices is to focus on the spiritual part of ourselves. That is to live in the world without belonging to the world. We belong to our spiritual self, our soul. This implies an effort to descend with our mind into our heart and stand there in the presence of God. Visualize yourself ready to dive into a warm swimming pool. Let this pool be divine power and plunge yourself in the soothing waters of divine presence. Feel the warmth of the water and let go of yourself. You will not drown, for the water will sustain you. Your worries and concerns will be eliminated, your body will be lighter, and your spirit will take over and rejuvenate you. Now you have a new companion, your spiritual self. Martin Buber completes this image with his famous words: "The world is not divine play, it is divine fate." Our existence has divine meaning. Creation happens to us, burns into us, changes us, we tremble and swoon, we submit. We participate in creation, we encounter the creator and offer ourselves as helpers and companions. We cannot experience our spiritual self with scientific methods. We need simply to *take in* God with each breath that we breathe. Without oxygen we die; without the breath of the spirit, we cannot live spiritually.

We belong to a world of worries, entangled in an endless chain of urgencies and emergencies. What would really happen if we decided to connect with God-within, our inner self, our spirit? We can speculate that nothing external would happen: no applause, no music, no praise, no artificial amenities. But we might begin to sense a sort of quietude, a joyful feeling of gratitude for being alive, a state of inner harmony, a yearning for love. The continuous experience of love, serenity, happiness, joy, effectiveness, perceptiveness, and wisdom that you have had only in bits and pieces can now be available to you all of the time as long as you remain mindful of divine presence. You will learn how to experience the world as a friendly, loving place that has been designed to give you everything that you need. You will develop a "miraculous dimension" in your daily life. Beautiful things will happen in such an order that you can no longer ascribe it to mere coincidence. You will experience an energy emanating from within that will make things possible for a life of fulfillment and joy.

Spirituality means the ability to find inner peace and happiness in an imperfect world and to feel that one's own personality is imperfect but acceptable. From this peaceful state of mind come both creativity and the ability to love unselfishly, which go hand in hand. Acceptance, faith, forgiveness — letting go of wrongs and injustices — peace, and love are the traits that define spirituality.

I cannot argue with the rationalists about the power of spirituality as a therapeutic tool. I do not need to. Some day therapists and clients will be surprised by the joyous discovery: a human being is a spiritual entity, but we must open ourselves to the spiritual experience to know this in our depths.

"Is there any better truth about ultimate things?" asks Carl Jung. "Nobody can know what ultimate things are. We must, therefore, take them as we experience them. And if such experience helps to make your life healthier, more beautiful, more complete, and more satisfactory to yourself and to those you love, you may safely say: 'This was the grace of God.'"

Once the illusion that we are masters of our own fate fades, we turn to a Superior Power for sustenance. It is in God that we find unconditional love and comfort. Prayer, a communion with God, seems to make its presence in the most unexpected places. In hospitals and medical schools, on college and university campuses, Americans seek solace in prayer. Before each cardiac surgery, the team of heart specialists of Loma Linda University Hospital offers a prayer invoking God's presence and guidance. I have been an eyewitness to this practice over a hundred times.

Psychiatry no longer dogmatically labels religion the infantile longing for the all-powerful parent. Psychiatrist Arthur Kornhaber adds prayer to his conventional therapy with troubled adolescents at the St. Francis Academy in Lake Placid, New York. "To exclude God from psychiatric consultation," says Dr. Kornhaber, "is a form of malpractice. Spirituality is wonder, joy, and should not be left in the clinical closet."

Personally, I use prayer in my practice. Either before clients come or after they leave my office, I offer a prayer that our therapeutic relationship may be directed toward desired healing. I pray that I might have clarity of mind to understand the clients' problems and that they in turn may incorporate the insights gained during the therapeutic hour.

In most of my clinical work these days I am aware that the *change* that my clients are looking for is not coming from any particular intervention that I formulate. Rather, my connection to God, the divine presence in my daily life, catalyzes clients' connection to their own sense of divine presence. A widening circle of rapport permeates the therapeutic hour; the individual or the family experiences a warmth and acceptance in my presence as they interact with me or each other, like a healthy contagion that heals my clients and nourishes me.

Thoughts to Ponder

- In your spiritual quest, some groundwork will enable you to connect with your soul. This includes a belief that you are more than your physical self.

- The most important feature of your personality is not your physical appearance; it is your spiritual presence, the invisible part of you that supports and sustains the visible.

- As you experience the external world, like the bee who searches to extract honey, you search to extract what is good and beneficial to your inner world.

- When you experience an event that leaves you with a good feeling, cherish it as much as you can.

- A challenge: Can you stop thinking too much about your worldly self — how to dress, where to eat, what to buy, where to go for entertainment?

- Is there a retreat, a special place within your own home, where you can find yourself comfortable to be in communication with yourself?

- When you schedule your daily activities, work, responsibilities, and play, appropriate a few minutes for introspection — a time to collect your thoughts, refine them, and become aware of your inner needs.

- As your body attains maturity, what can you do to help your maturing spirit?

Chapter 19

Who Is Normal?

> The "normal" man bites off what he can chew
> and digest of life, and no more. Humans aren't
> built to be gods, to take in the whole world; they
> are built like other creatures, to take in the piece
> of ground in front of their noses. God can take
> in the whole creation because He alone can make
> sense of it.
>
> — *Ernest Becker*

To be *normal* is a splendid ideal for the unsuccessful, for all those who have not yet adjusted to life and living. For people who have far more ability than the average, for whom it is never hard to gain successes and to accomplish their share of the world's work — for them, restriction to the normal signifies the bed of Procrustes, unbearable boredom, infernal sterility, and hopelessness. There are many people who become neurotic because they cannot achieve what they perceive to be the normal, as there are people who are neurotic because they are hemmed in by their perception of the normal. Carl Jung recognized these underlying aspirations as some of the reasons for neurosis.

Being normal or being happy are perceptions, like beauty in the eyes of the beholder, which vary from person to person. In our daily deliberations we try to do what we think is the "normal" thing to do. Or we try to be happy according to our emotional and physical needs.

When we ask, What is normal? or the corollary to the question, What is mature? we find that all definitions are ultimately inadequate.

We have difficulty accepting and recognizing that there is inner fragmentation of the self. Trying to keep the fragments together causes tension. Fulfilling only one fragment of the self leaves the rest unfulfilled. It is only through harmonization of all parts that the mosaic of our personality is realized. Of what, then, consists a normal person?

As you evaluate yourself, your physical appearance, your thoughts, feelings, actions, and interactions with your environment, and you feel reasonably satisfied, then basically you are a normal person. You have the ability to survive, to meet life's realities, to become closer to others, to be creative and productive, and to harmonize your inner qualities with the world outside you.

Attaining the *normal* is an ongoing process that requires effort, energy, and will. Normalcy can also be determined by what the individual can bear to tolerate beyond set standards. It is not fixed externally. It is what an individual can tolerate in deviation from the norm.

Roberto Assagioli, in his book *Psychosynthesis*, proposes the theory of harmonization. He emphasizes that it takes five steps to adjust harmoniously and integrate the existing aspects of our personality. The five steps are: Recognition, Acceptance, Coordination, Integration, and Synthesis. A sixth step I have found significant in my practice is Parenting.

Recognition: Recognizing most aspects of personality is hardly ever a problem. However, it takes more work to find the less obvious qualities and deal effectively with them. Suppose you become aware of a situation where *envy* emerges within and reaches an acute stage. Several times you notice this aspect of yourself. If you let envy continue, the process of integration becomes difficult. The sooner you recognize envy and understand its influence, the sooner you can minimize the conflict and foster harmony with the other aspects of your personality: "I am not just envious, I am also alive, strong, intelligent," etc.

When you habitually compare yourself with other people, you spoil things for yourself. You are trapped by your unfriendly comparisons. However, you can find your way back to harmony if you choose to look into other facets of your personality. Waste no effort agonizing over jealous comparisons. Go back to your original state of being, *the creator you were meant to be.*

Focusing on one aspect you have already chosen to work with provides that aspect with energy. If you preoccupy yourself with the envious part of your nature, with the emphasis on the existing state of things rather than on the *changes* you wish to see happen, the result is an increased difficulty without altering the situation. Labeling yourself "jealous" tends to accentuate jealous behavior. If you feel more alive when you are involved in a jealous interaction, then your identity is built upon this trait, and to abandon it brings the threat of disintegration.

Having recognized one aspect of your personality, you can move on to concentrate on two — perhaps those that seem more central or more important at the moment. No choice should be made in a rigid way. Be open and flexible to honor and recognize a new emerging attribute of your personality that needs to be heard for a reason. A light touch, common sense, and a healthy sense of humor often supply the best guidelines for integration.

Acceptance: If we accept that there are negative parts that prevent growth, we can eliminate them. Acceptance and coordination of all our traits often turn out to be complementary processes that help each other to proceed with increasing momentum and lead to the integration of each aspect within the personality as a whole.

By rejecting in ourselves a part that we perceive as undesirable, we cut it off from the direct energy line it needs. This creates a block and causes it to seek energy indirectly by manipulating and generating conflict. It then develops in a one-sided, distorted fashion, increasingly at odds with the rest of the personality. In essence, denying certain undesirable parts of ourselves is just as detrimental as total identification with a single trait.

When we first recognize new attributes, our *attitude* toward each of them — as toward people — varies. In each case our attitude is determined by many factors, two major ones being our personal *values* and our *self-image*. We tend to accept a quality, whether positive or negative, that we consider good and useful according to our value system. We tend to reject another that we see as bad, harmful, or useless. However, a person possessed by jealousy may more easily accept a *bad* trait and have considerable difficulty accepting a *good* one. Aspects that are consistent with our self-image are easily accepted. Those that do not fit our image are usually rejected.

When qualities of one's personality are repressed, they cannot be integrated — perpetuating unmet needs and frustration. When they go unrecognized, they want everything. Just a little attention is often all they need. A little bit of satisfaction goes a long way.

What choices do you have when your emerging attributes are many? If there is a part in you that makes the demands of a four-year-old, you cannot ignore it. This part in you makes demands because it has not really been *satisfied* since you were four years old. As you start paying attention to it, feeding it, caring for it, it will grow up. Soon it will want to do more mature things, more in tune with the things *you* want to do. So gradually you bring it in, and it becomes a part of you.

Coordination: As we explore a neglected area of our personality, we discover that the *core* of this area is basically good. If this part is demanding or negative, it is so because it was denied the opportunity of expressing itself. A basic purpose of the coordination phase is to find acceptable ways in which to satisfy and fulfill a need that has surfaced into recent awareness. Having sufficient understanding of each part of our personality, we can satisfy it and incorporate a new facet of personality into an emerging new identity.

You are faced with a demand by a part that prevents you from making a decision. Suppose that you cannot satisfy this demand. Can you at least say, "Well, I can't really give in to this, but is there something else I can do instead?" By asking such a question, you do not ignore the need or demand, but rather, you honor it.

You may discover within yourself a five-year-old child who wants to be loved. "How do you want to be loved?" you ask. "Twenty-four hours a day, seven days a week," is the response.

Well, you cannot fulfill that request, but is there anything else you can do?

You can say, "I understand that you want to play all the time. You are important to me, but I also have other things I want to do. So I would like to play with you an hour a day. Let's try it for a week and see how it works." So you make an agreement with that part of your personality that appears demanding; it is a compromise by which you do not ignore that part of you. You give it recognition, and you also involve that part when you are about to make a decision.

Christine was dealing with a *controller* part of herself. She wanted to be in control and to rule everyone in sight, to get them under her thumb — beginning with herself. Basically, she did not want all that control. I asked her to consider the controller and start a dialogue with it.

CONTROLLER: I want you to do all I ask all the time.

CHRISTINE: Why do you want that? Why?

CONTROLLER: Because I am insecure and afraid.

CHRISTINE (WITH EMPATHY): What else are you?

CONTROLLER (IN A SAD VOICE): I'm weak, very weak and hungry.

CHRISTINE: If you stop controlling me, I will feed you.

CONTROLLER: It's not just food I need.

CHRISTINE: What else?

CONTROLLER: I want love and care.

In developing this sort of dialogue, Christine became aware that the *controller* part in her needed loving attention. Not knowing how to ask for love directly, it turned to control, and with control it tried to force others to do all sorts of things, hoping they would act as surrogates of love. I asked her to continue with her dialogue.

CHRISTINE: I can't let you run my life. I can't let you manipulate me. But I see your need. I'll be very glad to love you.

CONTROLLER: I really don't want to control; I just want love.

Of course to be able to respond lovingly, you must recognize, accept, and understand the different parts of your personality in depth, as good parents understand their children. It is very hard to love crying, demanding children. However, once you see that they are desperate for love and don't know how else to go about getting it, loving them becomes possible.

The very core of the negative parts of our personality will surprise us by its positive aspects. *Nothing good without its equivalent bad,* and *nothing bad without its equivalent good.* It relates to the old Socratic truth that individuals do not choose to do something bad if they see clearly that they have a choice between something bad and something good. But sometimes we are not able to see.

Integration: Once we discover the various aspects of our personality, the challenge remains: how can we coordinate and integrate all these in order to function physically, emotionally, and mentally as a *whole* person?

Visualize yourself in front of an orchestra and ask: How can I get harmony out of all these instruments? If you are not a conductor, it will be difficult. But you are in charge of your personality, and conducting all its parts is not impossible.

Conflicts arise when a part of your personality is denied expression. Then, through manipulation and devious maneuvering, it seeks fulfillment. As it becomes stronger, it is able in unusual circumstances — such as moments of stress and decision — to take possession of the entire personality. Perhaps there is a minimal awareness during these moments. It is in retrospect that we see and are baffled by our own damaging impulses. We are blind to them when they surge to the surface. Initially, we interpret the new behavior as our own — a behavior taking on increasingly undesirable aspects that we are unable to stop. In the earlier example of Christine, when the controller was dominant and the loving part was emerging, she identified with the controller. When she first became aware of the loving part of her personality, she probably interpreted its sensitivity as weakness to be ignored. But as the loving tendencies became stronger, manifesting themselves through fantasies or affecting her actual decision-making process, she eventually became increasingly concerned. The inner conflict reached the conscious stage. For a while she might have kept pushing away the new tendencies, thereby making it much harder to deal with. Or she might have decided to understand what was really happening, either by herself or with the help of a therapist.

But suppose that one of the attributes wants to stay in control. Then the conflict is fully open and raging. The individuals who identify with only one aspect of their personality, claiming, "I'm a controller," or "I'm a lover," deny other parts of themselves. They find either of the identifications increasingly difficult to maintain and gradually become more *identified with the conflict* — they are in a state of ambivalence. However, the increasingly uncomfortable position demands a resolution of the conflict, a reconciliation of the two opposing parts.

In many conflict situations one part strives to have control all the time, inhibiting the expression of the other parts. When this is the case, you can never be fully present in an activity, nor can you enjoy it or be fully effective in it. For example, we might have a part that wants to work all the time — the *compulsive worker* — at war with one that wants to celebrate life and enjoy it to its fullest: let's call it *Zorba*. When we are trying to work, Zorba intrudes, making us feel tired, getting in the way of concentration, and enticing us with fantasies of drinking and dancing or lying in the sunshine of the Aegean Islands. But when we finally have time and freedom for leisure, the compulsive worker, unwilling to have us do anything but work, fights back, nagging at us with thoughts or worries about work and making it impossible for us to relax and enjoy our leisure.

In such a situation, once the parts are recognized and accepted, it is usually possible to start a dialogue with them from the position of the objective observer. Have them recognize that fighting one another for control has led to a dead end, a stalemate, in which *both are losing out.* You can then suggest a compromise where both parts agree to take turns at being in control, undisturbed, for a reasonable time. Sometimes it is quite obvious how the time should be shared: the compulsive worker's space clearly is on the job; Zorba takes over in leisure time. In some cases, a change in the daily routine may be necessary. Definite periods of leisure may have to be scheduled if your busy life does not provide for them. The improvement in quality and in effectiveness of work is likely to make up for the decrease in time.

Synthesis: Time-sharing is perhaps the easiest approach to integration and may appear downright simplistic, but in practice it is surprisingly effective. A *temporary* compromise fosters further coordination of the parts involved, leading to a closer form of cooperation. Understanding the reasons for the conflict and the needs of parts involved often shows that, through cooperation, both parts can achieve their goals, and each can do so more fully than if each was on its own. As two or more parts are recognized and fulfilled, they move closer together. Through coordination and cooperation, they are drawn more and more toward each other. Eventually, a merging of the two occurs. If the two are at about the same level of development, the merging is an actual fusion that results in a more complete *new part*. If one is considerably more developed than the other, it will take the smaller one *inside itself*. The more developed one will preserve much of its own original identity, but in its new form its coordination, effectiveness, and range of expression will be greatly improved.

In Christine's situation, the integration of the controller and the loving parts could result in a controlled lover or in a loving controller. Or a completely new part could result from the synergistic effect of the fusion. Christine's unrealistic control and her devious maneuvering to attain love, having opposite effects, balanced out each other's excesses when fused, leaving available energy — a healthy outcome. Love comes to us on its own merit, provided we are lovable and capable of loving.

This interplay of the various attributes of our personality, their refinement and synthesis, give new dimensions to our life and to our interaction with other human beings. With a sense of responsibility for managing the balance of power among aspects of the self, we become caring, loving, and cooperative. Integration of all aspects of our personality leads to our harmonious interaction with others, with humankind, and with the world.

Parenting: Realizing the ever-emerging parts of my own personality, the inflowing forces with their positive and negative qualities, I find myself using the metaphor of parenting. Regarding myself as a benevolent parent helps me develop a fairly constructive style that is consistent and easy to follow.

Perceiving myself as a parent makes me responsive to the different aspects of my personality as if they were my children, dependent, infantile, needing my care and support.

Thinking as a good parent tends to satisfy my grandiose delusions that I am "superdad." I can comfort my children, help them recognize what they are, and give them the attention they need.

Parenting, of course, tends to be difficult when I try to meld together several children in my family, my personality. I teach them to tolerate not being the only child or at least not being singled out for favoritism. They have to cooperate and accept each other's presence.

As a parent, I have to make decisions. My parts, by now a fully trained team, have played for many years; some games they have won and some they have lost. I have to add to my parenting the qualities of a coach. Here rises the difficulty — I have no magic to make them a winning team. But as a good coach, I must know the strengths and weaknesses of each player. I know when to put one on the bench and when to call one into play according to his or her talents. They have to respect me so that I can lead them to optimize their chances of winning. Some decisions are good; others are not so good. Team effort is necessary.

In Genesis, we read: "And God said, let us make man...." Although there is but one God, cooperative effort was necessary for the creation of man — "let us make...." You have that same choice, the privilege of saying to yourself, "Let us decide," thus involving all parts of your personality.

"We" is the superparent I wish I were and am sometimes expected to be. We can battle out a conference on this harmonization process while the children listen, ask, watch, integrate, rebel, or cooperate.

Thoughts to Ponder

- Who is "normal"? What does "normal" mean? I suppose it means conforming with or constituting an accepted standard, model, or pattern. You may want to conform with an accepted standard, or you may choose to be who you are. Make the changes that you wish to make in yourself, and live life creatively.

- Be spontaneous. Growth is creative, and creativity, one of our most powerful endowments, requires freedom and willingness. Freedom and spontaneity require risk.

- It is your nature to become what you were meant to be, although currently you may not know what that is. What you were meant to be has no fixed limits, only the limits you impose upon yourself. In exploring your individual potential, shape yourself into a complete, useful, and happy person.

- Keep track of your initiative. Your body cannot move, stand up, or sit down simultaneously. Each movement is either on a clear command out of your own initiative, or you move at the initiative of another person. Do you wish to initiate your own action, or do you prefer to take direction from others?

Chapter 20

Pan Metron Ariston

One is rich not through one's possessions, but
through that which one can with dignity do
without.

—*Epicurus*

If a man is moderate and contented, then even
age is no burden; if he is not, then even youth is
full of cares.

—*Plato*

I wrote this book not to replace psychotherapy or any other
form of therapy and therapeutic system. My current effort has
been motivated by and based all along on my faith that *healing power* lies within each individual. Answers to the manifold
problems of life exist within each person and can be realized
as we wrestle genuinely with alternatives and options that are
available.

Men and women make choices in life, pick goals and pursue them, each one according to his or her needs. Sometimes
they discover that this life does not bring them the satisfactions
it promised, that it does not meet totally their inner needs and
desires.

Are there any other choices? Of course there are, but no one
would dare to impose on us a new choice. We may have to discover this new choice ourselves. Many of us try for a life of
pleasure and success, or for a life of adventure and novelty or
of intellectual superiority. Others simply aim for a life of living and loving and having fun, making friends and establishing
meaningful relationships, in marriage or not, having children

or not, but still living like human beings. They can take time to watch the sky, to see the trees and smell the flowers, eat a good meal, enjoy the company of a friend, have a picnic, even care about other human beings and have them care in return. This does not mean they cannot have some success and fame as well, or simply some recognition, and even earn some wealth. But we do not need to be rich or successful to live a good life as a human being.

Good life? Yes, everyone is entitled to a good life. We should look at ourselves often, re-examine and re-evaluate our total being, a little every day. It is not difficult to discover that there is a life for us. Whatever that life may be, we have to define it, but we need to make a choice that lies within our current reality.

The late Dr. Herbert Holt proposes three choices, without judging any of them as good or bad.

> We can choose the world of money, prestige, and power, which beckons with material rewards, glamor, and excitement.
> We can choose the world of self, insulated and isolated, whose only lines of communications are with fantasy and daydreams.
> Or, we can choose the interpersonal world of the self in relationships with others and the modest rewards that love, friendship, and concern for another can bring.

We are able and free to pick any of the above choices, provided we realize that each choice has its own value and price. A mature adult must be willing to pay whatever the choice costs.

If we choose as our goal glory, money, prestige, and power, we cannot expect a sense of *enoughness*. There is no such thing as enough glory or enough money. Bottomless is the well of the human desire for more. In an urge to achieve these we may have to invest a lifetime. Then we cannot expect to be loved for ourselves or to experience the warmth of friendship.

If we choose the glamor of fantasy and magical thinking, chasing after unrealistic goals, stumbling and hurting ourselves and others in the dark corridors of daydreaming, we cannot expect to stabilize in the real world, to be accepted and find peace. We cannot expect others to follow our fantasies or to be our friends and respect us.

But if we pursue the world of reality and shape our lives

after the humble human condition, maintaining an honest approach and a healthy attitude toward others, we might discover our own humanity in relation to another human being. We might discover the power of love and friendship.

Pan metron ariston is a most profound and important adage handed down from the ancient Greeks. It has been mistranslated as "Nothing in excess." A more accurate translation would be, *Every measure that one takes with caution, proves excellent.* Experienced and wise teachers throughout the ages have admonished their followers to apply *moderation in all things:* whatever you do daily, don't overdo it; keep a balanced life. Excess has rarely made anyone happy. In view of the universal agreement that the principle of moderation enjoys, it is amazing that there is so much excess in the world. To a degree, we are all victims of the "more" mentality.

We have some savings in the bank, but we want more. We have a car, but it would be nice to have another one, perhaps a bit more sporty. We have a house, but we would like another one for vacation time or even for an investment. There is no end to our wanting more, and mass media remind us in striking advertisements that we need more to feel happy. Our society tends to impress excess upon us by seeking to create desires that we automatically translate into needs.

Visualize yourself pushing a shopping cart in a supermarket. You are planning to buy a few supplies. Wandering in the aisles are other shoppers dropping groceries into their carts, reading labels, and picking up items that, all of a sudden, you think you might need. Mesmerized, you load up your cart with produce that you originally had no intention of buying. Momentarily, you suffered from a "more-itis" attack, the disease of wanting more.

Well do we know that a person can eat and drink only so much, sleep so long, run so far, work so hard, worry so much, spend so much money, expend so much energy, enjoy so much pleasure, or endure so much pain at any given time. Yet we are all conditioned, either culturally or genetically, to seek excess. The phrase "I would like" becomes "I must have," whether it be more money, food, drink, gadgets, or even more love.

You are at a restaurant. While you are savoring your cocktail, into your mind comes the thought: This drink is so good, I must have another one. And just as you begin eating your lunch, another thought occurs: I'm going to have that good dessert to-day. Our minds are attuned to seeking more. Yet we know too well that even things that are basically good become bad and harmful when used to excess. The principle seems to hold up under all circumstances — from another piece of cake, to another drink, to another cigarette, to ideals such as happiness, love, power, patriotism, success, freedom, and security.

If we consider the meaning of moderation and live by the concept of having a bit less, life will be most rewarding. Happiness will be easier to attain, for it will be with us all the time. When you wake up in the morning, it will suffice that you are alive; you did not die in your sleep. You take a shower, have breakfast, dress, and go to work. You are alive…and, as a matter of fact, since you are alive, each day brings you some choices that will make your life a little more pleasant. There is no prescription for the pursuit of happiness, neither from others nor from materialistic possessions.

Do you want more love? If yes, how much more? Perhaps as a child you wanted unconditional love. You probably expected everybody to love you. Then it was important; you needed all the love you could get to survive emotionally. As an adult, however, before you receive any love, you must learn to be lovable and able to give love. You don't have to overpower your loved one, doing cartwheels to demonstrate your love. Your loved one may suffer emotional paralysis if you love him or her to excess. Moderation in loving and being loved can be very effective.

How much power do you need? Perhaps some power over your personal life, a charge over your well-being, is important. But suppose you want more; you want to rise to eminence through ambition, hard work, or the call of duty. Soon you will notice that the more absolute is your power, the more envied or even hated will be your lot — and, of course, the more a prisoner you will be of your own traps. The web catches the spider. You can no longer wander at leisure in the streets and parks of your own town or sit on a lonely beach listening to the waves and watching the sea gulls against the sunset. While you enslave others to your services, you will become the most miserable of slaves.

Does moderation apply to patriotism? Plato made an interesting observation: The most glorious and admirable virtue is to love one's own homeland. I have a problem with this sort of wisdom. Nothing in excess, but simple respect must be given for the preservation of the natural world, the soils and waters and air that make up the earth and the atmosphere. Nothing in excess, but an attitude of caring must be developed, caring about life and living on this unique and fragile planet. Nothing in excess, but serious concern must be shown for the earth's resources, which, while enough for normal and sensible human needs, are not infinite and can soon be despoiled.

How much *success* is enough for a person? For a company? For an organization? Alan Watts claims that "nothing fails like success." A person who thinks that a series of successes will provide happiness is in a state of hypnotic hallucination. The well of success is bottomless. Success gives us, temporarily, some satisfaction, and then we seek another success to maintain ourselves in the illusion of happiness. Yet when success is a cooperative effort, most of the participants derive lasting satisfaction from each other.

What shall we say about *freedom* and *security*? Is there such a thing as unlimited freedom? As for security, nothing is more secure than insecurity itself. Regardless of how secure we become in all aspects of life, we are still imperfect human beings and, therefore, insecure.

The suggestion *pan metron ariston*, moderation in everything, represents a sane message for our tormented planet. In accepting this message, people around the world would benefit in every aspect of their existence. Moderation is the only promising hope. People in power, whether in governments of nations or in leadership of the various faiths and institutions, must get control of themselves to forgo the temptation of using deep public fears and hatreds for limited political purposes. Rather than an orgy of political power, leadership should take on the constructive initiative of education. Nations and people can unlearn the bad habits of excess, selfishness, and greed and learn to design their destinies, to think with reason, to act with respect.

It is a liberating feeling when we become aware that we do not need an excessive amount of everything to be happy. What each individual needs is a personal awareness of having enough, a rational spirit that knows our needs are not as many as mass media would have us believe. If we are ever to experience some relief in this world with its crazy passions, we must temper our irrational wants.

How do I know that the concept of moderation would work? Because it could all begin with me. It could begin with you. Will it guarantee a happier life?

Once you have read the last paragraph of the last page of this book, sit back and rest. Close your eyes or, better yet, take a nap.

On waking up, think through aspects of the book that you still remember. You may go back and re-examine them. Some idea, some concept may have impressed you.

You are worthwhile merely because you are alive, you are human, and you have potential. You may feel relatively insignificant, yet you are responsible for your actions, your words, your thoughts, your feelings, and your choices. You can change almost anything that makes your life uncomfortable or unhappy. How? Delving into your own self will bring awareness of who you really are, as opposed to what you have been told or conditioned to believe you should be. Once you have an awareness of your inner truth and you accept your self, you will discover a channel to your goal.

In the course of your growth, if you have learned to feel unworthy, you can re-educate yourself to feel differently by constructively utilizing what is already yours — your thoughts, actions, and movement processes. Rooted within yourself is the source of all influence. Nothing can stop you from rearranging your own life. You have the emotional and spiritual ingredients. You are equipped with intelligence, energy, and ability to live fully and independently. When you refuse to live self-reliantly and are discontented, envying others or comparing yourself with others, you will feel a sense of misfortune. However, the moment that you relinquish the tarnished self-image that you may have inherited from your parents, teachers, and peers and decide to do everything that you possibly can for yourself emotionally, physically, and socially, your life will take a new turn.

Now that you have come to the end of this book, give yourself some credit for your patience and perseverance in coming this far in your reading. It is an accomplishment to finish a book. My sincere hope is that as you traveled with me you found the treasure that exists in every human psyche. In so doing, you have discovered your own potential, strengths, and vulnerabilities, possibilities that comprise human nature. You will be surprised by the amazing results that you will have once you implement a few of the ideas and directives that you gleaned from this reading. Occasionally you may go back to certain pages and read over paragraphs that have made some impact upon you. But above all, you will be reassured that beyond any therapy and beyond any recovery the potential of healing, growth, and maturity exists within. You are the potential. I want to wish you well in your endeavors and in your personal journey in self-fulfillment and happiness.

DESIDERATA

Go placidly amid the noise and the haste, and remember what peace there may be in silence.

As far as possible, without surrender, be on good terms with all persons. Speak your truth quietly and clearly; and listen to others, even to the dull and ignorant; they too have their story.

Avoid loud and aggressive persons; they are vexations to the spirit.

If you compare yourself with others, you may become vain or bitter, for always there will be greater and lesser persons than yourself.

Enjoy your achievements as well as your plans. Keep interested in your own career, however humble; it is a real possession in the changing fortunes of time.

Exercise caution in your business affairs, for the world is full of trickery. But let this not blind you to what virtue there is; many persons strive for high ideals, and everywhere life is full of heroism.

Be yourself. Especially do not feign affection. Neither be cynical about love; for in the face of all aridity and disenchantment, it is as perennial as the grass.

Take kindly the counsel of the years, gracefully surrendering the things of youth. Nurture strength of spirit to shield you in sudden misfortune. But do not distress yourself with dark imaginings. Many fears are born of fatigue and loneliness.

Beyond a wholesome discipline, be gentle with yourself.

You are a child of the universe no less than the trees and the stars; you have a right to be here.

And whether or not it is clear to you, no doubt the universe is unfolding as it should. Therefore be at peace with God, whatever you conceive Him to be.

And whatever your labors and aspirations, in the noisy confusion of life, keep peace in your soul.

With all its sham, drudgery and broken dreams, it is still a beautiful world. Be cheerful. Strive to be happy.

Appendix

A Growth Model

The following model is based on the precept that each human being is endowed with the greatest power in all creation. This inner power, known as *dynamis,* from which the word "dynamic" is derived, is the central force for human growth.

As we grow physically, mature emotionally and spiritually, and produce in ways that are fulfilling, we feel good. Our self-esteem is high, and we succeed in areas that we choose. No matter how creative or noncreative we are, the inner longing for growth is there waiting to be realized.

At times, driven by pain, overcome by desire, exhilarated by hope, alone or with our families or peers, we search endlessly for relief and resolution. In the process, we may have to fight or manipulate our environment in order to grow. If the meaning of growth is distorted, we may seek power, control, or money in the pursuit of happiness. Real growth implies ability to survive emotionally and physically, to become close to others, to be creative and productive, and to make sense and order out of the world outside of us.

This model will present you with familiar precepts; however, basic steps to enhance your well-being, whether you are in therapy or out of therapy, are always valuable.

Although authorities may improvise answers to life's dilemmas, each of us may expedite matters by observing our own behavior and adopting a healthy attitude. This process can be started as of this moment, unless the reader is severely psychologically impaired. The following precepts can be instrumental in discovering a life philosophy and our own potential.

1. Observe the Mischief Monger

Events in your past may victimize your present. Ruminating on your unfortunate childhood and bitter past experiences are indulgences you cannot afford. These can poison your present life, stifle your creativity, and paralyze you emotionally. The mischief monger may give you an excuse to rationalize your situation on the basis that unalterable damage has been done to you by your parents or some other adults who are responsible for your failure. Undoubtedly, your parents may have contributed to your insecure feelings and your bad self-image. But if you continue to blame others, your symptoms will also continue to contaminate your present life. An attempt to rise above your early misfortunes and replace them with healthy activities may prove more advantageous. Remember, you may not have been responsible for what happened to you when you were a child, but you are responsible for perpetuating neurotic patterns in the present. Say good-bye to the mischief monger and to your yesterdays; release yourself from the chains of childhood.

2. Beware of Nagging Stressors

Every time you experience stress, tension, or excessive fear, check your thoughts. Is the cause of your stress the current situation you are in? Has something that happened to you in the past just come into your mind? Are you fearing that something bad will happen in the future? Once you identify the origin of your anxiety, you will be in a better position to handle it. If you trace the source of your pain, you will not feel so helpless. At least you will be able to seek some new direction.

Identifying your nagging stressors can motivate you to scale back commitments, reorganize priorities, and do whatever it takes to reduce pressure. Most humans are resilient in the face of stress, once they have identified the cause. Getting to the root of your stress helps you regain a sense of control. Feeling in charge of your life is the key to coping with all pressures.

3. Tolerate Anxiety

Although you may have had years of therapy or you may have successfully graduated from it, a certain degree of tension or anxiety is to be expected. All persons have to live with some anxiety and tension, and these may precipitate various symptoms from time to time. You are no exception. Some anxiety and tension are inherent feelings of humans. When you begin to get anxious, slow down and try to figure out what is troubling you. If you are unable to resolve your tension entirely through self-observation, try to involve yourself in some physical activity that will take your mind off your current situation. Move out of your tense environment for an hour. Take a walk. Go swimming. Visit a friend. Keep a journal of self-observation to gain objectivity and clarity of thought.

4. Deal with Anger

Periodically, all humans have to live with a certain degree of anger. It is normal; from time to time you will feel some resentment. If you explore the reason and become aware of the reason for your anger, most likely you will avoid converting it into physical symptoms. Excessive and undefined anger often results in chronic headaches, stomach ulcers, colitis, arthritis, and, of course, a most unhappy existence.

Permit yourself to feel angry if the occasion justifies it; but express your anger in proportion to what the situation merits. Expressed anger may not be resolved anger; however, in recognizing that it exists, you may choose to engage in a muscular exercise to provide an outlet for aggression that is not destructive to you or others.

5. Tolerate Frustration

Instant gratification is appropriate for infants. It is unlikely that, in our adult life, we can ever obtain full gratification for all of our needs. It is important to realize that we can derive a great deal of joy out of life if we learn to accept that less than 100 percent of our needs will be met. Expect to be frustrated to some extent and learn to live with it. Frustration may cause you to take charge of your life and seek new directions. Furthermore, frustration may sharpen your skill at problem solving or provide viable options in your current life.

6. Correct Elements That Can Be Corrected

In your life situation, try to figure out how to correct whatever appears correctable. Lay out a plan of action. You may not be able to implement this plan entirely, but do as much of it as you can immediately, and then routinely keep working at it. The walk of a thousand miles begins with the first step, claims a Chinese proverb. No matter how hopeless things may seem, if you apply yourself you can do much to rectify matters. Do not get discouraged. Don't curse the darkness; light a candle.

7. Adjust to Irremediable Situations

No matter how much you try to rationalize a tragedy in your life and find comfort, the pain is there and you feel it. You may have to adjust to an amputation, or you may have to learn to live with a handicapped spouse or the loss of a child. There are certain evils in life — war, famine, disease, death — that we all have to cope with; there are certain situations from which we cannot escape. It takes a good deal of courage and character to live with adversity and pain. If we start feeling sorry for ourselves — Why me, Lord? — we are bound to be upset. We cannot respond to trouble like a weathervane. We try our best to remedy the trouble. If we cannot, we will have to adjust to it, minimizing what seems to be bad and concentrating on something good in our lives. It takes courage and character to live with our troubles, but as we look around, we notice that there are others who are suffering more than we are. You may remember the old saying: I complained that I had no shoes until I met a man who had no feet.

8. Observe Destructive Activities

At times we are our own worst enemy. We embark upon situations that cause unnecessary pain. You would think we would learn something from a bad experience. But, no. We go back to it, repeat the performance, and get hurt again. If you have a notion that a situation is bad for you, try to divert yourself from acting it out. Use your willpower. Suppose you got a ticket because you violated the speed limit. A week later, you are on the same road and suddenly recollect the experience. The policeman comes to your mind, causing you a tinge of anger, and a sudden urge for revenge surfaces in your mind. The road is clear. I'm going to go faster, you say to yourself. In your eagerness to defy the law, you miss the stop sign. No policeman is around, but another car that has the right-of-way smashes you broadside. Accident! It is a compliment to you as a person if you can catch a glimpse of yourself and regain control when destructive tendencies propel you to behave immaturely. When you sense that you are about to do something crazy, stop in your tracks and figure out what you are doing. Can you face the consequences responsibly?

9. Do Not Make Unreasonable Demands on Yourself

Living in a highly competitive world, we subject ourselves to a *success syndrome*. We want to succeed at any price to satisfy the ambition of our parents, to keep up with our neighbors or rise above them, or to achieve greater independence and stature. Reality assures us that all people have their assets and liabilities. Chances are that you may not be able to accomplish what some persons can do, and there are some things you can do that others find impossible. Of course, if you are determined and try hard enough, you can probably do the impossible. Unquestionably, you will pay a price — exhaustion and hard work. But you can still live up to your creative potential and get joy out of life without wearing yourself out.

10. Examine Your Self-Image

Most of our failures in life originate with a devalued self-image. My book *A New Self-Image* speaks extensively on the matter of what it takes to restore a positive sense of self. Here let me point out that at times we utilize self-devaluation to bolster our helplessness and, perhaps, to nurture dependency. If you have a tendency to devaluate yourself as a result of all the degradation you have endured, you may be using self-devaluation as a way of punishing yourself because of guilt, or you may be seeking to make people feel sorry for you, or you may be trying to attract attention through bemoaning your ill-fate. All people are different; every person has a uniqueness just as every thumbprint is unique. The fact that you do not possess some qualities that other people have does not make you inferior. You know your life can be better, but it takes effort to make it so. Taking the easy way out — expecting a miracle, a good fairy, a rescuer to come to your aid — results in frustration and an unhappy existence. It is with determination and effort that you can learn to rely on your own strength and live a happier and healthier life. Evaluate your good qualities and make a simple plan for yourself to use them constructively. What about your negative qualities? You can keep those under control until you are able to deal with them in a nondestructive way.

11. Derive Some Joy out of Life

God created us for joy and fulfillment. Both these goals require work and effort. Focusing on trouble and difficulties can deprive us of joy, which is our right as humans. If we try to minimize the negative, the bad aspects of life and living, and concentrate on the good and useful things, our experiences in our daily lives will be more rewarding. It is important for our mental and physical health that we reap the maximum pleasures possible each day. Living on recriminations of the past and on future forebodings, we make our lives strenuous. Simply stated, we must concentrate on achieving happiness in the here and now. Stage a pleasant hour or day for yourself and experience life's free-given joys.

12. Adjust to Your Current Situation

Whether you are male or female, at this time of your life you may have to adjust to your present life. Whether you are single or married, husband or wife or parent, as an adult you have to relate to others with a sense of responsibility and flexibility. Though you may feel emotionally disturbed, dependent, immature, hostile, hypocritical, inevitably you have to fill your part as completely as you can. Suppose you have a conflict with your boss, which leaves you with destructive feelings toward him or her. Instead of adopting an attitude that may result in the loss of your job, you may consider understanding the forces that serve to disturb you. This may be a time for you to test your marketability, to develop options, just in case you find yourself unemployed. While you are in search of another job, you may make an effort to keep the relationship going in a way convention dictates so that you may continue in your employment. A practical way of trying to get along with people is to attempt to put yourself in their position and to see things from their point of view. At any rate, try to recognize what is going on in your life and correct matters that may be resolved and adjust to those that cannot be changed. If you are able to evoke good feelings rather than negativity in people, you should be able to move on with life and living without too much difficulty.

By reviewing the above twelve precepts once a week, you will gradually make them your personal property, and you will follow them automatically.

Bibliography

It is with gratitude that I acknowledge the following books and with confidence I recommend them to the reader.

—P.M.K.

Angyal, Andras. *Neurosis and Treatment: A Holistic Theory.* New York: John Wiley & Sons, 1965.

Assagioli, Roberto. *Psychosynthesis.* New York: Viking Press, 1971.

———. *The Act of the Will.* Baltimore: Penguin Books, 1974.

Becker, Ernest. *The Denial of Death.* New York: The Free Press, 1973.

Beecher, Willard and Marguerite. *Beyond Success and Failure.* New York: Simon & Schuster, 1975.

Bloomfield, Harold, and Robert Kory. *The Holistic Way to Health and Happiness.* New York: Simon & Schuster, 1978.

Booth, Leo. *When God Becomes a Drug.* Los Angeles: Jeremy P. Tarcher, 1991.

Butterworth, Eric. *Discover the Power within You.* New York: Harper & Row, 1968.

Durckheim, Karlfried. *The Way of Transformation.* London: Unwin Paperbacks, 1988.

Dyer, Wayne. *You'll See It When You Believe It.* New York: Avon Books, 1989.

Fromm, Erich. *To Have or to Be.* New York: Bantam Books, 1981.

Gendlin, Eugene. *Focusing.* New York: Bantam Books, 1981.

Hoffman, Bob. *No One Is to Blame.* Palo Alto, Calif.: Science and Behavior Books, 1979.

Holt, Herbert. *Free to Be Good or Bad.* New York: Evans & Company, 1976.

Jung, C. G. *Memories, Dreams, Reflections.* New York: Vintage Books, 1965.

Kalellis, Patricia. "The Narcissistic Personality." Unpublished paper. Mountainside, N.J., 1981.

Kalellis, Peter. *Wedded or Wedlocked?* Canfield, Oh.: Alba House, 1979.

——. *On the Other Hand.* Allen, Tex.: Argus Communications, 1980.

——. *A New Self-Image.* Allen, Tex.: Argus Communications, 1982.

Keen, Sam, and Anne Valley-Fox. *Your Mythic Journey.* Los Angeles: Jeremy P. Tarcher, 1989.

Kopp, Sheldon. *Guru, Metaphors from a Psychotherapist.* Palo Alto, Calif.: Science and Behavior Books, 1971.

——. *An End to Innocence.* New York: Bantam Books, 1978.

Krishnamurti, J. *Freedom from the Known.* New York: Harper & Row, 1969.

——. *Beyond Violence.* New York: Harper & Row, 1973.

Kushner, Harold. *When All You've Ever Wanted Isn't Enough.* New York: Summit Books, 1986.

Larsen, Tony. *Trust Yourself.* San Luis Obispo, Calif.: Impact Publishers, 1979.

Lasch, Christopher. *The Culture of Narcissism.* New York: Warner Books, 1979.

Lechman, Judith. *The Spirituality of Gentleness.* New York: Harper & Row, 1987.

LeShan, Lawrence. *Alternate Realities.* New York: Ballantine Books, 1977.

Levinson, Daniel. *The Seasons of a Man's Life.* New York: Ballantine Books, 1978.

Lindbergh, Anne Morrow. *Gift from the Sea.* New York: Vintage Books, 1975.

Maltz, Maxwell. *The Search for Self-respect.* New York: Bantam Books, 1973.

May, Rollo. *Man's Search for Himself.* New York: Signet Classics, 1967.

Miller, Alice. *Prisoners of Childhood.* New York: Basic Books, 1981.

Miller, Stuart. *Men and Friendship.* Los Angeles: Jeremy P. Tarcher, 1983.

Moore, Thomas. *Care of the Soul.* New York: HarperCollins, 1992.

Morrison, Douglas, and Christopher Witt. *From Loneliness to Love.* Mahwah, N.J.: Paulist Press, 1989.

Moustakas, Clark. *Loneliness and Love.* Englewood Cliffs, N.J.: Prentice-Hall, 1972.

Watts, Alan. *This Is It.* New York: Vintage Books, 1960.

Wheelis, Allen. *How People Change.* New York: Harper & Row, 1976.

Wood, Garth. *The Myth of Neurosis.* New York: Harper & Row, 1987.